Exegesis of the Soul:
Three Treatises on the Nature,
Origin, & Destiny of the Human Soul
PAPUS

Exegesis of the Soul:
Three Treatises on the Nature, Origin,
& Destiny of the Human Soul

by
PAPUS

The Human Soul Before Birth & After Death (1898)
How is the Human Being Constituted? (1900)
What Becomes of Our Dead? (1914)

Translated and Introduced by

Tau Phosphoros
Archbishop and Patriarch
Apostolic Church of the Pleroma

TriadPress
Hainesville, IL

Exegesis of the Soul: Three Treatises on the Nature, Origin, & Destiny of the Human Soul
by Papus

Translated and introduced by Tau Phosphoros
First English Edition

Published 2022
Copyright ©2017, 2022 Tau Phosphoros
All rights reserved.

ISBN: 978-1-946814-00-5

Triad Press, LLC
260 E. Belvidere Rd. #357
Hainesville, IL 60030

Exegesis of the Soul

Translator's Introduction vii

THE HUMAN SOUL BEFORE BIRTH & AFTER DEATH

INTRODUCTION 7
I. Analysis of the Pistis Sophia by Mr. E. Amélineau 8
II. The Universe 11
      Messenger of Death. The Inhabitants of The Invisible World. The
      Celestial Plane.
III. Man 14
      Constitution of Man. Spirit of Imitation. Origin of the Soul.
      The Soul After Physical Death. The Soul of the Non-Repentant and
      Non-Initiated Sinner. Evolution of the Soul of the Initiate.
      Clarification on the Receivers.
IV. Jesus and Initiation 23
      Creation of Christianity. Incarnation of Jesus. The Virgin Mary.
V. It Is From The *Virgin Of Light* That Is Issued Mary The Mother Of Jesus 24
      Incarnation of the Spirit of Jesus. The Twelve Apostles.
      Role of the Apostles. The Two Vestures.
V. The Key of the Salvation of the Incarnate Soul, or the Evangelical Initiation .. 27
      Role of Jesus. I Have Come to Bring Division. Render to Caesar.
      The Initiate on Earth. Sayings of Jesus. Path of Initiation.
      Theurgy. The Total Reintegration.
VI. Tables and Keys 33
      Repentances of Pistis. Interrogations. Alphabetical Table. Of
      the Pistis Sophia.
VII. General Conclusion 40
Notes 43

HOW IS THE HUMAN BEING CONSTITUTED?

Primordial Question 47
The Three Principles 48
The Trinity in the Physical Being 49
The Physical Body - The Astral Body 51
The Three Psychic Centers 55
Various Classifications of the Principles 62
Conclusion 69

WHAT BECOMES OF OUR DEAD?

Introduction 73
The Familial Fortress 74
Chapter I: Section of the Eagle 75

    Feminine Intuition - The Ideal
Chapter II: Section of the Man 77
    Constitution of the Human Being. Death and the Evolution of
    the Three Principles. The Human Mind and its Evolution
Chapter III. Section of the Lion 84
    The Notion of the Planes. The Forces in the Three Planes.
    Communications Between the Various Planes. Experimentation.
    Union of the Visible and the Invisible. The Errors and Traps.
    Active Faith and Prayer.
Chapter IV: Section of the Bull 91
    What is Death for the Philosopher? The Dead are voyagers,
    momentarily absent. Death for one's country frees the spirit
    at once from all suffering.
Epilogue 94
The Young Soldier 95
Notes 96

Exegesis of the Soul

Translator's Introduction

Exegesis of the Soul is a collection of three short, but excellent works by Papus discussing the nature of the human condition, especially the origin and fate of the soul, the seat of human consciousness. The works collected here are: *The Human Soul Before Birth and After Death, How is the Human Being Constituted?*, and *What Becomes of our Dead?* These three works, written over a period of some sixteen years, show the depth of understanding of the human faculties and constitution held by Dr. Gérard Encausse, known within the esoteric milieu as Papus. His mastery of the occult, or hidden, side of man was so thorough that he was able to seemingly effortlessly translate very advanced and sophisticated philosophical concepts into the popular language of the day. Like all hierophants who dare to lift the veil of Isis, or part the curtain of the Holy of Holies, there were some who would accuse him of coarsening the occult science. But while Papus may indeed have been the *vulgariseur de l'occulte*, that is to say the popularizer of the occult, he was never a profaner of the occult. His mystical insight was second to none, and his expositions of the timeless doctrines of the esoteric tradition are as valid and pertinent today as they were over a hundred years ago.

In *The Human soul Before Birth and After Death*, the earliest of the three works, published originally in 1898, Papus looks at the teachings of the *Pistis Sophia*, which had only recently been translated into French for the first time by Amélineau. He gives a summary of the work and relates it to the initiatic tradition. This is a rare example of Papus addressing the Gnostic doctrine in particular. While he is well known for his works on Martinism, esoteric Freemasonry, and the occult tradition in general, we do not often find him writing on Gnosticism proper. But we must recall that at the time of this writing, Papus had been a bishop of the Eglise Gnostique for six years; and it is interesting to note that this work appeared a year before Tau Sophronius produced his Catechism which was largely based upon the *Pistis Sophia*. It must also be remembered that not many Gnostic texts were extant at this time. The Nag Hammadi discovery would not be made for nearly fifty years, and of the few small collections which existed at the time, much had not even been translated. Because of this dearth of source materials and reliable historic information, some erroneous notions prevailed at the time. For example, at the time, the authorship of the *Pistis Sophia* was attributed to Valentinus himself. Most scholars today would not make this claim. Nevertheless, this is a small thing and does not detract from the value of the exegesis. If there is any criticism to be found here, it is that the originally published edition of this work does not always make clear which portions constitute direct citations from the *Pistis Sophia* and which are Papus' commentary or paraphrase. But context makes this clear in the majority of the cases. It should be noted that the page numbers given when referring to the *Pistis Sophia* are referencing the original Amélineau translation.

How is the Human Being Constituted?, published in 1900, explores esoteric anatomy and physiology, as well as the non-corporeal elements of man. Much of what is contained in this work will be familiar to Martinist initiates, but the present study goes much further than what is introduced in the standard Martinist curriculum. Here, the "bon docteur" makes easily comprehensible the complex interplays between the functions of man on the various planes of existence. He even goes so far as to cross-reference his own system of terminology with the nomenclature of other teachers and traditions, so that one approaching this study from a different background will easily be able to integrate and assimilate what otherwise may have seemed as irreconcilable. Some of the analogies used by Papus will seem greatly outdated, with references to horse-drawn carriages and telegraphs, but that is merely an accident of the era in which he lived. Technologies are constantly changing and evolving, but the principles that they demonstrate are fundamental to the cosmos; timeless and unchanging. The same analogies could be made today using computers and wireless communication technologies as illustrations, but the principles they represent would be identical. The traditional tripartite division of man and nature makes these concepts very easily adaptable to Gnostic philosophy as well as to alchemical theory. For the keen student, Papus gives the keys to the reconciliation of various philosophical doctrines.

What Becomes of our Dead? was written in 1914, at the outset of the Great War. There is somewhat of a somber mood that runs throughout the work, as Papus attempts to convey the real situation of the human soul and its course through life, death, and the afterlife; all while taking on a comforting and consoling tone for those who are losing so much, yet simultaneously making a point of not giving false hope to the desperate. He is truly seen in his role as the "good doctor" here, giving a clear and honest analysis while maintaining a deep compassion for his fellow human beings. This short work is divided into four principal sections: Eagle, Man, Lion, and Bull, which cover the constitution of man, the nature and development of thought and the mental faculties, and the continuity of consciousness.

Taken together, these three works offer a rich overview of the origin, purpose, and destiny of the human soul. For neophyte and hierophant alike, these works are a wealth of knowledge and insight that hold up to multiple readings, offering surprising revelations upon each return. The study of these succinct and erudite treatises will show the reader why Papus is one of the most universally respected esotericists of the belle époque and since. Ever seeking to embrace that which unites and shunning that which divides, Papus stands out as a great unifier of esoteric movements and reconciler of occult doctrines. Many of his dreams are yet to be realized, but it is our sincere hope that with the works of Papus put into publication in the English language, he will find more emulators willing and eager to take up his worthy mission.

April 23, 2017
Tau Phosphoros
Patriarch
Apostolic Church of the Pleroma

Exegesis of the Soul

THE HUMAN SOUL
BEFORE BIRTH & AFTER DEATH

CONSTITUTION OF MAN AND THE UNIVERSE
KEY OF THE GOSPELS, EVANGELICAL INITIATION

according to the
PISTIS SOPHIA

by
The Doctor PAPUS

Doctor in medicine, Doctor in Kabbalah, Director of
the Faculty of the Hermetic Sciences
President of the Supreme Council of the Ordre Martiniste
Officer of Public Instruction

With four figures and explanatory tables of the Pistis Sophia

---

> The one whose spirit will be intelligent,
> I do not impede at all; but I exhort him
> all the more to tell the meaning which
> has incited him.
> - Words of Jesus, according to Valentinus
> (*Pistis*, p. 62)

1898

Exegesis of the Soul

To
Dr. Nizier PHILIPPE
of Lyon
To the one who is justly called
by the *Vox Populi*
THE FATHER OF THE POOR AND THE PRISONERS
This study
is respectfully dedicated
by THE AUTHOR

Exegesis of the Soul

GRAND GENERAL TABLE - KEY OF THE PISTIS SOPHIA

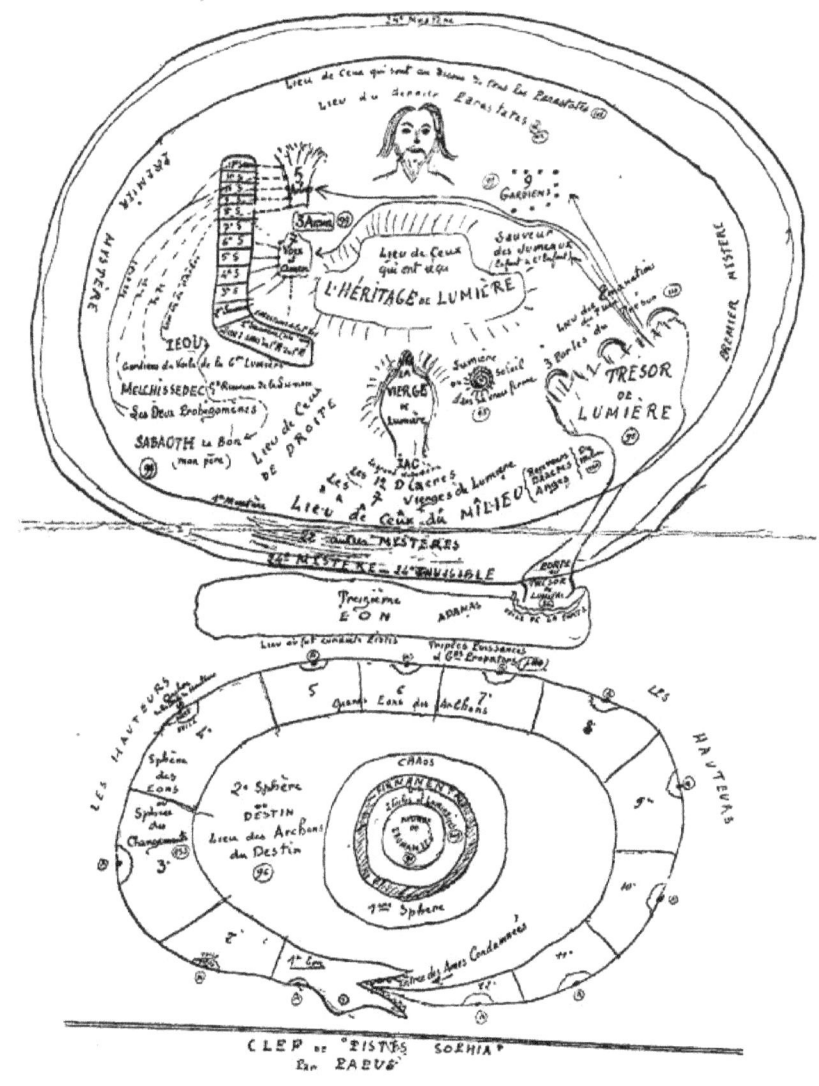

INTRODUCTION

The French translation of the Coptic manuscript of the *Pistis Sophia*, by Mr. E. Amélineau, has a singular importance for the diffusion of Christan spiritualism.

However, the very importance of this work requires some clarifications without which the work remains truly closed; for it is an initiatic work, and composed in such a way that the initiates alone could comprehend its secrets.

Mr. E. Amélineau, in a very scholarly introduction, has considered the work from a critical and historical point of view. He has thus fulfilled his duty as scholar and conscientious translator. But there *lacks a key* to the work which allows it to be recognizable in the descriptions of the astral plane and the celestial plane that Valentinus gives us. It is this key that we have endeavored to find and to bring down to the level of our readers: but within a certain limit.

This marvelous work may be read in four manners and reveals four meanings for each of the ideas set forth. To make a complete commentary on the *Pistis* would require several volumes. Thus have we restrained our ambition to the clarification of the natural meaning of the revelations of Valentinus. This work alone has required several months. Later, we will perhaps approach a new plan of exposition. But for the moment, we are going to limit ourselves to the following points:

1. Brief analysis of the *Pistis Sophia*;
2. Summary of the constitution of the Pleroma, or physical and hyperphysical Universe according to this work;
3. History of the Involution and Evolution of the human soul before and after terrestrial life;
4. Light on Christianity and the Gospels, with the help of selected citations, and explained where it is necessary;
5. Dictionary of the principal subjects treated with references to the French Edition.

This will be made in such a way that it is complete by itself, and that it constitutes for the reader a collection such that it is not absolutely necessary for him to procure the original work. But we hope that our key will help greatly the serious student who, possessing the work of Valentinus, has been rebuffed until now by the studied repetitions and calculated obscurities that the writer has employed in order to hide, in the era of the appearance of his work, what we have the duty to attempt to reveal in our era.

However, let "those who know" be reassured. As much as it is required to shed the brightest light upon the primary meaning of the works of this genre, so do I know what prudence is necessary concerning the second and third meanings which touch on the very mysteries of the celestial plane.

Be that as it may, we are convinced that the translation of the *Pistis Sophia* will allow all Christians, without distinction of church, to grasp the profound and traditional sense of the Gospels.

I

Analysis of the Pistis Sophia by Mr. E. Amélineau (p. iv to vii of his translation).

As in all the known Gnostic works, and we know of at least four, the revelation of the marvelous Gnosis, the knowledge of which placed the fortunate possessor in a position infinitely advantageous for obtaining the eternal blessing after death, is put into the mouth of Jesus resurrected from among the dead.[1] The author of the *Pistis Sophia* affirms to us that, after his resurrection, Jesus spent eleven years teaching this admirable Gnosis to his disciples and to the gathering of women who followed him. When the first scene of the book opens, Jesus is seated upon the Mount of Olives with all those who surround him, the twelve apostles, Mary his mother, Mary Magdalene, Martha, and Salome (it is at least the principal actors who will grasp the words in proportion to the view opened by initiation).

Scarcely are we set on the place where some of the following scenes are going to take place, that Jesus, seated a little apart from his disciples, is surrounded by a great light which serves to clothe him and raptures him into the heavens in the middle of the terror of the cosmic elements. The disciples are dazed and stupefied at the sight of the light which has enraptured Jesus. They make their prayers heard and Jesus returns to them to explain the mysteries that he can and must explain to them. He explains to them first that he has gone to his father; that the vestment of light that has been brought to him on the Mount of Olives was the same one that he had laid aside in one of the Aeons when he descended to earth. He set out from there in order to explain to them certain words of the Gospel and certain preparatory acts to his descent upon the earth, like the coming of Elijah in the person of John, the Annunciation of Gabriel to Mary, and the election of the apostles as a result of the placing of superior souls into their bodies at the moment of conception. Then, all at once, without any transition, and, it must also be said, without the least detail of the book indicating a lacuna, it narrates his ascension into the superior mysteries of the Aeons. In these various mysteries of the various Aeons, the chiefs or archons of each place, the guardians of the doors, and all the inhabitants of the Aeon traversed, made way in his presence, astonished, stupefied, dazed, constrained by the magical words with which is covered the vestment of light which is upon Jesus. But Jesus, in some of these Aeons - and there again there is an interruption in the narrative without there being any lacuna in the text - withdraws only after having inflicted a chastisement upon a certain number of their inhabitants. The archons, in fact, in his sight, have wished to combat the light which clothes him; they have been punished for it by the removal of a third of the light which was found in them, by the changing of the revolution of their spheres which will then turn to the left instead of turning to the right, which throws the greatest confusion into the horoscopes that drew able men to the earth, which led to their entire confusion when they did not know about this change, and when they operated at any time as if the astral movement had continued, when for six months it was to the left and for six months to the right, but which did not at all prevent their practices from being found just when the movement corresponded to the original notion, which took place for half the year.

By a rather painful transition, Jesus, upon an interrogation of Mary Magdalene, explains how the souls would have had to wait, in the Aeon in question, until the number of perfect souls had been fulfilled, then how these souls have been created, how they have shared the fate of the spheres whose revolution had been changed inversely, and there Jesus enters again into a continuation of the first subject that he had treated. It is then that Pistis Sophia appears, the Aeon whose misfortunes and salvation are going to be recounted at length in the work.

This Pistis Sophia was one of the twenty-four superior emanations. Gazing on high one day, she saw the light "in the firmament of the great Treasury of the Light." She wished to reach into this place and stopped practicing the mystery of the place that she inhabited. She sung a hymn to the light that she had seen. But, instead of being heard, she was only able to incur the jealousy and hatred of these who shared her dwelling; they pursued her, she fled outside of her Aeon, fell into the depths of the dark chaos and there found herself exposed to all the attacks of the archons of this chaos, and of those which existed below. These archons created through emanation a multitude of bizarre beings who had as their mission to steal from Pistis Sophia the luminous part which existed in her. She was then plunged into all the horrors of the darkness, and exposed to all the attacks of the diverse and horrible emanations created in order to fight her. But, if her trials were great, her courage was even greater: she did not lose confidence at all, she turned towards the light and addressed to it a hymn of *repentance*, as expressed in the text. This *repentance*, as well as the following twelve, are modeled on the Psalms applied to the various states through which she passes, and, in order to render the thing more visible, the disciples, men or women, give its explanation by reciting precisely the Psalm on which the *repentance* has been modeled. At the ninth repentance, Sophia is heard; Jesus, the Savior, is sent to her and draws her by degrees from the miserable state where she is found, then saves her finally from the chaos. The repentances are then changed into thanksgivings. Jesus leads her below the thirteenth Aeon and leaves her there while advising her to call him, when the time comes that certain archons will wish to mistreat her. This time arrives when Jesus is in the world of men, on the Mount of Olives. Jesus then went to her aid, just as he had promised her, and he introduced her into the thirteenth Aeon. Meanwhile, after the thirteenth repentance of *Pistis Sophia*, and in the middle of the explanation of her first hymn of thanksgiving, the text is all of a sudden interrupted by a page inserted on the verso of folio 114, and contains a theme entirely outside of those that we have found up to here. Then, on folio 115 recto, is this title: second volume of *Pistis Sophia*, and this second volume opens with the continuation of the previous explanation, namely the explanation of the first hymn of thanksgiving pronounced by Pistis Sophia.

After Pistis Sophia has been reintegrated into her Aeon, the book changes pace, or to state it better, the interrogations, which had sometimes been encountered in what precedes, become as a general rule from this moment. These interrogations bear at first on certain particular points of the constitution of the invisible worlds, then they turn nearly entirely upon the eschatological problems and the different cases that they raise for the various categories of souls. I will not devote myself to analyzing them here; the reader will find them at length in the work that I have translated. What it will suffice me to indicate, is that salvation will correspond after death to the degree of initiation received by the souls; that the sinful and non-initiated souls may be saved by the faithful; that the sinful and initiated souls are condemned to be lost irrevocably, without anything being able to save them.

I also ought to add that one of the dominant traits of the Valentinian eschatology in the *Pistis Sophia* is the possibility of amending a first bad life by a second better one, for the disciples of Valentinus and Valentinus himself perfectly admitted metempsychosis.

Here again, the explanations that Jesus gives to his listeners are suddenly interrupted by a title thrown into the middle of the development: *A part of the books of the Savior*. The passage thus announced comprises two sheets; it is not related, far or near, to what precedes it or to what follows, and the third sheet from this title is the continuation of the explanations interrupted so inopportunely, it seems. These explanations are continued by the examination of the new cases that the disciples raise in this eschatological moral of Valentinianism; they give a place for Jesus to describe some of the particularities of the Valentinian Hells, until the moment when a new direction of the work is announced by the title of *Extract from the books of the Savior*. This part is no more complete, it seems to me, than the others. It is Mary Magdalene who speaks in the final lines, and her phrase does not seem complete to me.

With the *Extract from the books of the Savior*, I will say, the Gnostic work takes a new direction. The beginning shows that it is an entirely unique book that we have here, for it begins with these words: "It happened then, after they had crucified Our Lord, that on the third day he was raised from the dead." As in the other books that I have already indicated, the disciples gather near to the Savior, on the banks of the Sea, and address a prayer to him to which Jesus responds by explaining to them the situation of the planets, after having led them to his right. These planets are five in number: Saturn, Mars, Mercury, Venus, and Jupiter. They are governed by the last in which is placed Sabaoth the lesser and the good. Then, at the request of Mary Magdalene, Jesus explains what are the *middle paths* which are likewise five in number, each of which has for overseer archons whose names are given; names as completely bizarre as the forms of these archons. Then Jesus dismisses the left-hand virtues to the place that they are to occupy. Pressed anew by his disciples, he responds to them that he is going to confer upon them the baptism of the Remission of sins, and, indeed, confers it on them. After having thus conferred this baptism, Jesus tells his disciples that there are other baptisms, and he undertakes the explanation thereof. The explanation is cut off by a lacuna of eight sheets; there is without doubt a paper which has been detached from the original manuscript and which has been lost. When the text resumes, it continues the eschatological explanations begun beforehand, and it gives certain cases where metempsychosis will take place, according to the position of the planets in the various signs of the zodiac. Then the book ends abruptly in the middle of a phrase where the disciples deplore the unfortunate fate of the sinners. I do not believe, for my part, that it had ended in this way, and I am convinced that the final pages have disappeared.

The true conclusion of the work is found shortened, in one page which is attached at the end of the manuscript: it speaks of the dispersion of the apostles, three by three, to the four cardinal points, to preach the good news of the Gnostic Gospel; Christ confirming their preaching by signs and wonders, such that the entire earth know the kingdom of God.

INTRODUCTION

The French translation of the Coptic manuscript of the *Pistis Sophia*, by Mr. E. Amélineau, has a singular importance for the diffusion of Christan spiritualism.

However, the very importance of this work requires some clarifications without which the work remains truly closed; for it is an initiatic work, and composed in such a way that the initiates alone could comprehend its secrets.

Mr. E. Amélineau, in a very scholarly introduction, has considered the work from a critical and historical point of view. He has thus fulfilled his duty as scholar and conscientious translator. But there *lacks a key* to the work which allows it to be recognizable in the descriptions of the astral plane and the celestial plane that Valentinus gives us. It is this key that we have endeavored to find and to bring down to the level of our readers: but within a certain limit.

This marvelous work may be read in four manners and reveals four meanings for each of the ideas set forth. To make a complete commentary on the *Pistis* would require several volumes. Thus have we restrained our ambition to the clarification of the natural meaning of the revelations of Valentinus. This work alone has required several months. Later, we will perhaps approach a new plan of exposition. But for the moment, we are going to limit ourselves to the following points:

1. Brief analysis of the *Pistis Sophia*;
2. Summary of the constitution of the Pleroma, or physical and hyperphysical Universe according to this work;
3. History of the Involution and Evolution of the human soul before and after terrestrial life;
4. Light on Christianity and the Gospels, with the help of selected citations, and explained where it is necessary;
5. Dictionary of the principal subjects treated with references to the French Edition.

This will be made in such a way that it is complete by itself, and that it constitutes for the reader a collection such that it is not absolutely necessary for him to procure the original work. But we hope that our key will help greatly the serious student who, possessing the work of Valentinus, has been rebuffed until now by the studied repetitions and calculated obscurities that the writer has employed in order to hide, in the era of the appearance of his work, what we have the duty to attempt to reveal in our era.

However, let "those who know" be reassured. As much as it is required to shed the brightest light upon the primary meaning of the works of this genre, so do I know what prudence is necessary concerning the second and third meanings which touch on the very mysteries of the celestial plane.

Be that as it may, we are convinced that the translation of the *Pistis Sophia* will allow all Christians, without distinction of church, to grasp the profound and traditional sense of the Gospels.

I

Analysis of the Pistis Sophia by Mr. E. Amélineau (p. iv to vii of his translation).

As in all the known Gnostic works, and we know of at least four, the revelation of the marvelous Gnosis, the knowledge of which placed the fortunate possessor in a position infinitely advantageous for obtaining the eternal blessing after death, is put into the mouth of Jesus resurrected from among the dead.[1] The author of the *Pistis Sophia* affirms to us that, after his resurrection, Jesus spent eleven years teaching this admirable Gnosis to his disciples and to the gathering of women who followed him. When the first scene of the book opens, Jesus is seated upon the Mount of Olives with all those who surround him, the twelve apostles, Mary his mother, Mary Magdalene, Martha, and Salome (it is at least the principal actors who will grasp the words in proportion to the view opened by initiation).

Scarcely are we set on the place where some of the following scenes are going to take place, that Jesus, seated a little apart from his disciples, is surrounded by a great light which serves to clothe him and raptures him into the heavens in the middle of the terror of the cosmic elements. The disciples are dazed and stupefied at the sight of the light which has enraptured Jesus. They make their prayers heard and Jesus returns to them to explain the mysteries that he can and must explain to them. He explains to them first that he has gone to his father; that the vestment of light that has been brought to him on the Mount of Olives was the same one that he had laid aside in one of the Aeons when he descended to earth. He set out from there in order to explain to them certain words of the Gospel and certain preparatory acts to his descent upon the earth, like the coming of Elijah in the person of John, the Annunciation of Gabriel to Mary, and the election of the apostles as a result of the placing of superior souls into their bodies at the moment of conception. Then, all at once, without any transition, and, it must also be said, without the least detail of the book indicating a lacuna, it narrates his ascension into the superior mysteries of the Aeons. In these various mysteries of the various Aeons, the chiefs or archons of each place, the guardians of the doors, and all the inhabitants of the Aeon traversed, made way in his presence, astonished, stupefied, dazed, constrained by the magical words with which is covered the vestment of light which is upon Jesus. But Jesus, in some of these Aeons - and there again there is an interruption in the narrative without there being any lacuna in the text - withdraws only after having inflicted a chastisement upon a certain number of their inhabitants. The archons, in fact, in his sight, have wished to combat the light which clothes him; they have been punished for it by the removal of a third of the light which was found in them, by the changing of the revolution of their spheres which will then turn to the left instead of turning to the right, which throws the greatest confusion into the horoscopes that drew able men to the earth, which led to their entire confusion when they did not know about this change, and when they operated at any time as if the astral movement had continued, when for six months it was to the left and for six months to the right, but

Exegesis of the Soul

II

THE UNIVERSE

The Pleroma or Universe, physical and hyperphysical, is composed of *three worlds, of three planes* which are entangled and which we separate into figures for ease of description.

The superior plane, or celestial plane, is formed, for the author of the *Pistis Sophia*, of twenty-four concentric circles which he names the twenty-four mysteries[2]. The twenty-fourth mystery is the closest to the inferior worlds, and the first mystery is the most central. It is this first mystery that Jesus will describe in detail, and it is that which contains the heritage of the Elect, as well as the Force-Principles or celestial creatures.

The median plane, or astral plane of the Kabbalah, is represented by the dragon of Hermeticism, the ουροβορος (ouroboros) of the initiates, which forms a circle since the mouth devours the tail. This dragon symbolizes the *waves of fire* of the astral plane, the ocean of flames of the Hermetic initiation, and the Purgatory of the Christians.

The dragon is divided into twelve apartments or Aeons[3], each of these Aeons a gateway which opens to the superior world, "towards the heights," says the text. Each of these gates is hidden at the interior by a veil, and guarded at the exterior by an "astral spirit" or *archon*[4], which is called the Archon of the Gate of the heights. These twelve Aeons correspond to the twelve houses of the astrological zodiac. They serve as the place of trial of the condemned souls, and these latter enter into the various Aeons by the mouth of the dragon (entrance of the condemned souls).

The physical plane, or plane of corporeal humanity, is surrounded on all sides by the astral dragon. No being may come, therefore, from heaven to the material plane, or go from the material plane in heaven, without having to cross this domain of the dragon, this world of the archons filled with torments and traps. The physical plane begins with the firmament circle situated within the circle of chaos, and this physical plane contains the Stars and the Luminaries or Planets (p. 109) and, at the center, the world of humanity (p. 95).

In the account of Valentinus, these three planes are contained by another, from the world of humanity at the center, unto the first mystery at the periphery, and the celestial world goes even further (p. 102) with intermediaries between the various planes.

If we had followed this figure scrupulously it would have been nearly impossible for us to make understood the first mystery and its relation with the rest of the Universe or Pleroma.

That is why, in our general figure, we have represented the celestial plane apart from and above the other two, although normally it would envelop them. Between the celestial plane and the astral plane is found a place of transition, the thirteenth Aeon; between this thirteenth Aeon and the astral plane is again another place of transition where *Pistis Sophia* was led. Finally, between the astral plane and the physical plane exist various spheres (sphere of destiny, or second sphere, sphere of chaos, or first sphere) which indicate the planes of progressive materialization of the divine force.

Whoever reads the following translation will be stricken by the roles of the secondary agents called receivers. There are receivers of light or pacific receivers, and receivers of darkness. The role of these agents is to go seek out the souls at the moment they leave the body, to lead them across creation for three days and then to reunite them into the hands of those who are to reward or punish them.

MESSENGER OF DEATH

Ancient Egypt believed in a messenger of death who went to seek out the soul at the determined moment, and the work of ethics attributed to the scribe Khonson-Hotep speaks to us of it in a maxim that I am going to cite here:

"Place before you as a goal to reach an old age of which one may witness, so that you are found having perfected your house which is in the funerary valley in the morning to hide your body. Thus, when your messenger of death comes for you, to take you, may he find someone who is ready."

Moreover, a glance thrown on the general figure, and especially on the figure of the Pleroma, will allow one to fix well in the spirit this disposition of the worlds, and to resolve well any difficulties.

Let us now say some words on the inhabitants of these various worlds.

THE INHABITANTS OF THE INVISIBLE WORLD

The world of humanity is inhabited by souls clothed with bodies. As invisible beings, we will find here above all the *pacific receivers*, charged with receiving the soul at its exit from the body and carrying it to the astral plane, where it will find a multitude of beings with which it may have business.

These beings of the astral plane are above all the receivers of the archons, the archons of Destiny (p. 96), and the archons in all their functions. These archons are, by essence, enemies of the human soul, and they are particularly hostile towards it when the initiation does not allow it to be prohibited.

Exegesis of the Soul

THE CELESTIAL PLANE

The celestial plane first shows us receivers of the light, receivers of the middle, then a multitude of mysterious beings classified into three great centers: the middle, the right, and the left. This right and this left are not those of the figure, but those of the Christ of glory who occupies the center of the figure.

In the middle, we will find the Virgin of light charged with sealing the souls according to their elevation; then IAO, the great Hegemon; then the twelve deacons, the seven Virgins of light with the receivers, the deacons and the angels in the middle.

To the left, we find the sole gate by which heaven communicates with the other worlds. This gate unites the thirteenth Aeon with the Treasury of Light from where come the majority of the emanations which adorn the celestial plane. It is in fact from this Treasury of Light that are emanated the nine guardians and the Savior of the twins who are at the left of Christ, and the five trees, the three amens, and the seven voices which are *at his right*.

The five trees have each emanated, in their turn, a creative light.

The light of the first tree has emanated IEOU.

The light of the second tree has emanated *the guardians of the veil and the great light*.

The light of the third tree has emanated MELCHIZEDEK.

The light of the fourth and fifth trees has emanated the two PROHEGEMONS.

Finally, if we say that IEOU has emanated in his turn SABAOTH the Good, the one that Jesus called *his heavenly Father*, you will have the complete notion of the emanations which constitute this celestial plane, and that our figure will sufficiently clarify. To note also, however, the emanation of the twelve saviors derived from the five trees, and the twelve voices, let it suffice us to mention them, for their explanation would draw us outside of our subject.

III

MAN

CONSTITUTION OF MAN

It is provided with the previous particulars that the reader will easily be able to grasp the origin of the various principles which constitute the incarnate man.

Composition of the human being.

The human being, such as it is presented to us on earth, is composed thus:

1. A *hylic* or physical body.
2. An intermediary principle: *the spirit of spiritual imitation*.
3. *The immortal soul*.

To these principles must be added the non-incarnated forces, which are:

A. *Celestial Virtue*.
B. *Destiny*.

Let us speak on each of these principles.

The PHYSICAL BODY comes from the earth and will return there. It is formed by the principle immediately superior.

The SPIRIT OF SPIRITUAL IMITATION plays a large role in the work of Valentinus. It is the *principle of attraction down below*, the origin of the Satanic impulses which will attract the soul to the pleasures of matter.

The more the soul will have followed the impulses of this principle of evil, the more powerful will the bond which unites it to this principle be, and the more difficulty it will have in escaping the torments into which it will be drawn by this spirit of imitation which comes from the sphere of Destiny and which must remain there unless the soul succeeds in breaking the bond which attaches it to it.

The reader will observe too in the course of the eschatological part of the *Pistis Sophia* that it is often a question of a part of the human being called the *spiritual imitation*, such that, in the doctrine of Valentinus, man is composed of the body, the *spiritual imitation*, the soul, until this soul becomes pneumatic and blessed.

This *spiritual imitation* had the form of the body, born with the body, was attached to it for its life and followed it until death, witness of all the actions of the body and the soul, strongly reproaching this latter after its death and inducing it to sin during its life.

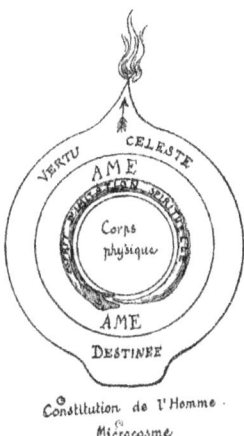

Constitution de l'Homme
Microcosme

Likewise, among the ancient Egyptians, man was composed of the body, the *double*, and the soul, which became blessed or spiritual after death, if it had been found just in the supreme judgment of Osiris. It is to the *double* that corresponds the *spiritual imitation*; the *double* was an attenuated image of the body, a more tenuous *imitation* of the body, more spiritual in a way, which was born with the body, growing with the body, dying with the body, then being revived without the body, thanks to certain magical ceremonies, and continuing to live after death in the place where the corpse was preserved.

SPIRIT OF IMITATION
(Analysis by the author of the Pistis)

"And the spirit of spiritual imitation makes the soul to bend and compels it to do all its iniquities, all its passions, all its sins, in a constant manner, and it remains different from the soul and its enemy, making it commit all these evils and all these sins. And it excites the pacific liturgies to be its witnesses in all the sins that it makes it commit. And even when it goes to rest in the night, in the day time it excites it through vices, or mundane desires, and it makes it desire everything of this world: in a word, it attaches it to all the works that the Archons have ordained, and it becomes the enemy of the soul, it makes it do what it would not wish to do.

"The spirit of pneumatic imitation separates Destiny and the body (the mystery of baptism) into one part, the soul too and the virtue it separates into another part. The very mystery of baptism dwells between the two."

Papus

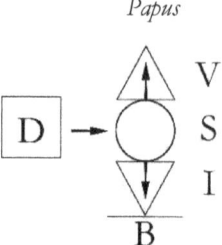

Incarnated Principles	S	Soul
	I	Spirit of Imitation
	B	Body
Non-incarnated Principles	V	Virtue
	D	Destiny

But to this center of attraction down below is opposed the *Celestial Virtue*, center of attraction towards the Upper and the Divine, origin of the *ideal* upon the earth, of the *pure desire* and of the regenerative *sacrifice*.

This celestial virtue comes directly from the *Virgin of Light* of the celestial plane; it will return there immediately after death and will remain tied for the whole terrestrial life to the soul in order to enlighten it and allow it to be lifted up by realizing the *Divine Love*[5].

The IMMORTAL SOUL, free to follow the impulses of the lower or the rapture of the higher, is sent to earth to *acquire initiation*. So long as it will not have penetrated the principle of creation, it will have to return to incarnate anew.

Destiny does not share in the human substance. Impassive spectator, it is there in order to stop the course of physical existence at the marked day, and, this done, it returns to the first sphere form where it comes.

The reader will now understand the following page which summarizes all this.

"When the infant comes into this world, *Virtue* is weak in it, the *soul* is also weak in it, and the *imitation* of the Spirit is weak in it; in short, the three are weak together: no one knows what it will be, either good or evil, and also the *body* is weak, and the infant eats the food from the world of the archons, and the *virtue* from the archons draws to it the part of the virtue which is in the nourishment[6], and the *soul* draws to it the part of the soul which is in the nourishment and the *spirit of spiritual imitation* draws to it the evil part which is in the nourishment with its desires, and the body too draws to it the insensible matter which is in the nourishment. As regards *Destiny*. it takes nothing from the nourishment because it is not mingled with it.

"Little by little the virtue, the soul, and the spirit of imitation become large, each of them lives according to its nature. The *virtue* exists in order to seek the light of the heights, the *soul* exists to seek the place of the justice which is mixed, that is to say that it is the place of mixture; *the Spirit of imitation* thus seeks all wickedness, desire, and all sins; the *body* feels nothing, except that it takes strength from matter," (p. 145 and 146).

ORIGIN OF THE SOUL

The soul of ordinary men draws its origin first from the very light of the archons, that is to say form the chiefs who exercise their power in the sphere of Destiny. So we understand the rage and the anger of these archons when the human soul comes to crush its creators of all superiority due to its valiant sufferings endured, and its personal initiation. Then the soul passes *as a shaft of fire* through the middle of the archons who recoil full of terror in their impotent hatred. All that the archons possessed of the divine, their light, their virtue, the very breath of their mouth becomes the substance of the human soul, while the tears of their eyes, the sweat of their bodies became the source of the animal souls. The distribution of the divine substance was ruled according to the astrological aspects. Such is the explanation of the magnificent following page[7].

"And when the time of the number of Melchizedek, the great receiver of light, had come, he went into the middle of the Aeons and all the archons attached in the Sphere and in Destiny, he carried off the luminous brightness from all the archons of the Aeons and from all the archons of Destiny, as well as those of the Sphere - for he took from them what troubled them - and it excited the Lord, who was their chief, to promptly have their arcs turned, and he carried off the virtue which was in them, the breath of their mouth, the tears of their eyes, the sweat of their bodies, and Melchizedek, receiver of the light, purified all these virtues in order to bear their light to the Treasury of Light, while the liturgies of all the archons gathered, the ones with the others, all their matter, and the liturgies of all the archons of Destiny with the liturgies of the Sphere, those which are under the Aeons, took them in order to make of them the souls of men, animals, reptiles, or savage beasts or birds, and to send them into the world of humanity.

"And furthermore, the receivers of the Sun and the receivers of the Moon, having looked at the heavens and having seen the figures of the progressions of the Aeons and the figures of Destiny and those of the Sphere, then carried away from them the virtue of the light, and the receivers prepared themselves to leave it until they gave it to the receivers of Melchizedek, the purifiers of light; and their hylic residue they carried into the sphere which is below the Aeons in order to make of it the souls of men and also that of reptiles, or animals, or savage beasts, or birds, according to the circle of the archons of that sphere, and according to the figures of its revolution," (p. 19).

THE SOUL AFTER PHYSICAL DEATH

Let us leave aside for the moment the role of the soul during the incarnation into the physical body; let us content ourselves with knowing that the aim of this incarnation is to acquire *initiation*, and let us occupy ourselves with the important question of the evolution of the soul after death.

According to the Kabbalah, the three principles of man each evolve by striving to regain their place of origin. The physical body returns to the earth, the aromal or astral body returns to the astral plane from where it came, and the immortal spirit endeavors to return to the center of its celestial origin.

This doctrine is going to be clarified in a very remarkable fashion by the following pages. We will see, indeed, that the soul of the initiate returns to the inheritance of the light after having left successively in their respective place of origin the Spirit of spiritual imitation and the Destiny. When the soul has been unable to acquire through initiation the knowledge of the sentences, symbols, and apologies which open the gates of the astral dragon of the terrible place of the Aeons, then the *Spirit of imitation* becomes accuser and tormentor, the black angel descended from the world of the angels of darkness seizes its victim and tortures it; but this torture itself *is never eternal.*

THE SOUL OF THE NON-REPENTANT AND NON-INITIATED SINNER[8]
Phases of post mortem evolution in general

Now, then, when the time will be fulfilled of this man, first comes Destiny, it will lead this man to death by means of the archons and their bonds, those by which they have been bound by Destiny; and then come the Pacific Receivers in order to lead away this soul outside of the body.

And then the Pacific Receivers remain three days to journey with this soul into all the places, leading it to all the Aeons of the world while Destiny and the Spirit of spiritual imitation follow this soul, and while the virtue withdraws to the Virgin of Light.

And after three days the Pacific Receivers lead this soul below, almost to the depths of the Hell of chaos, and when they have led it to the depths of chaos, they deliver it to those who chastise, and the Receivers withdraw into their place according to the economy of the works of the archons concerning the exit of the souls.

And the spirit of imitation becomes a receiver of the soul, it combats it, it returns it into each torment because of the sins that it has made it commit; it is therefore in great enmity with the soul.

And when the soul has finished the chastisements in the chaos according to the sins that it has committed, the spirit of imitation has it come out of the chaos, fighting it, reproaching it in each place for the sins that it has committed, and it leads it upon the path of the archons of the middle, and when it has arrived at them they introduce it (the soul) into the mystery of the Destiny, and, if it does not find them, they seek their Destiny.

And these archons chastise this soul according to its sins and what it deserves. And I will tell you the type of their chastisements in the emanation of the Pleroma.

If it happens, then, that the time of the chastisements of this soul has been accomplished in the judgments of the archons of the middle, the spirit of spiritual imitation leads the soul outside of all the places of the archons of the middle, introduces it into the presence of the light of the sun according to the order of the first man IEOU, and places it with the judge, namely the Virgin of Light. She tests this soul in order to see whether she will find it a sinful soul; she throws into it its virtue of light in order to maintain it with the body and with the union of the senses. Of all this I will tell you the type, when I speak to you on the emanation of the Pleroma.

And the Virgin of Light seals this soul, she charges one of its receivers to throw it into a body which is worthy of the sins that the soul has committed. And in truth,

Exegesis of the Soul

I tell you, she does not leave this soul in the changings of the body, without having given it its final age according to what it merited.

And of all this I will tell you the type, as well as the type of the bodies into which they throw them according to the sins of each soul; all this I will tell you when I will have finished telling you of the emanation of the Pleroma.

*Soul which has not listened to the spirit of spiritual imitation
in all its works*

Having become good, it receives the mysteries of the light which are in the second place, or even those of the third.

If the time of this soul has arrived to come out of the body, then the Spirit of spiritual imitation is added to this soul, as well as the Destiny; it is added to it in the path by which it will enter into the heights, and before it is delivered too far into the heights, *it tells the mystery of the dissolution of the seals and of all the bonds of the spirit of spiritual imitation*, the one that the archons have attached to the soul; and when it has been told, the bond of the spirit of spiritual imitation is dissolved and leaves it according to what has been said... and at once it becomes a great jet of luminous light, it traverses all the places of the archons and all the hierarchies of the darkness until it has reached the place of its kingdom of which it has received the mystery.

EVOLUTION OF THE SOUL OF THE INITIATE[9]

Likewise, a soul which has received the mystery in the first exterior place, if, after it has received the mysteries and accomplished them, it then returns and commits sin anew after the accomplishment of the mysteries and has not fulfilled the time when this soul is to come out of the body... and in that hour, the soul tells a mystery in order not to retain the Spirit of pneumatic imitation and the Destiny, to let it follow it, but without having the least power.

In this hour, the Receivers of this soul with the mysteries that it has received arrive; they seize this soul from the hands of the Pacific Receivers and the receivers withdraw into the works of the archons according to the economy of making the souls come out; and likewise the receivers of this soul, those which belong to the light, become wings of light to this soul, a vestment of light for it, and do not convey them into the chaos, *because it is not permitted to introduce into the chaos a soul which has received the mysteries*.

But they set it upon the path of the archons of the middle, and, when it arrives at the archons of the middle, the archons come before this soul, being in great fear and great trouble, with various faces, in a word, being in a great incommensurable fear.

And in this hour, the soul tells the mystery of their apology, and they fear greatly, they fall upon their face, fearing in the presence of the mystery that it has told and of their apology, and this soul and it abandon them to their Destiny while telling them: "Take your Destiny for yourself, I will not come into your place to set off from this hour, I have become a stranger to you forever; I am going to go into the place of my inheritance."

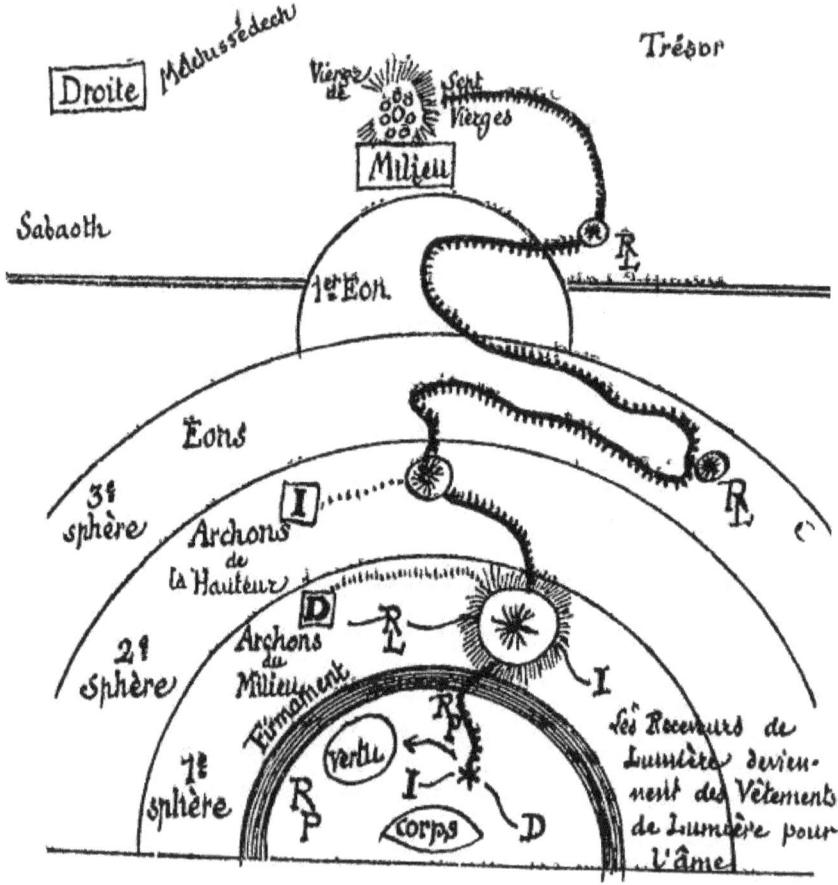

(Read 13th Aeon instead of 1st Aeon.)
The world is represented by a star in a circle.
R.P. - Pacific Receiver - R.L. Receivers of Light.
D. - Destiny - I. - Spirit of Imitation.

When the soul will have finished saying these words, the Receivers of Light will introduce it into the plane of the Destiny where it will give the apology of this place and of the seals that I will tell you about while speaking to you on the emanation of the pleroma. And it will give the Spirit of pneumatic imitation to the archons, and it will tell them the mystery of the bonds which have been attached to it, and it will say to them: "Take your Spirit of pneumatic imitation for yourself, I will come no more into your place to set off from this hour, I am a stranger to you forever." And it will give to each its seal and its apology. And when the soul will have finished saying these words, the receivers of the light will fly with it into the heights and they will introduce it into the aeons[10]; it will give to each its apology and the apology of all the places, the seals, and the tyrants of the king Adamas[11]; it will give the apology of all the archons of the left-hand places. And the receivers will introduce this soul anew to the Virgin of Light, and this soul will give anew to the Virgin of Light the seals and the glory of the hymns, and the Virgin of Light and the seven other Virgins of Light all test this soul, so that they all find their signs within it, their seals, their baptisms, their unctions; and the Virgin of the Lights and the receivers and the receivers of the light baptize this soul in order to give it the pneumatic unction. And each of the virgins of the light seal it with their seal, and the receivers ascend anew to the great Sabaoth the Good, who is near the gate of life in the place of those on the right, the one that they call the Father, and this soul gives him the glory of its hymns, of its seals, and of its apologies, and the great Sabaoth seals it with his seals, and the soul gives his knowledge and the glory of the hymns and the seals to the whole place of those who are at the right-hand; they all seal it with their seals, and Melchizedek, the great receiver of the light who inhabits the place of those who are at the right-hand, then seals this soul, and all the receivers of Melchizedek seal this soul, and Melchizedek introduces it into the Treasury of the Light. It gives the glory, the honor, and the glorification of the hymns with all the seals of all the places of the light, and all those of the place of the treasury of the light seal it with their seals, and it goes from there into the place of the inheritance.

The one, therefore, who receives the unique word of this mystery that I have told you, when he will have come out of the body of the matter of the archons, when the Pacific Receivers will have gone, when they will have unbound him from the body of the matter of the Aeons - for the Pacific Receivers are those who detach every soul which comes out of the body - when, therefore, the Pacific Receivers will have detached the soul which has received this unique and ineffable mystery, the one that I have just told you in the moment, then in this hour when it will be detached from the body of matter, it will become a great jet of light in the middle of these receivers, and the receivers will fear greatly in the presence of the light of this soul. They will fail, they will fall, they will cease at once to act through fear of the great light that they will have seen. And the soul which will have received the mystery of the ineffable, it will rise unto the heights, being a great jet of light, and the receivers will not be able to seize it, and they will not know what path it has taken, for it has become a luminous jet; it goes above, and no virtue may retain it in the least, nor may even approach it, but it will pass through all the places of the archons and all the places of the emanations of the light, and it will not pass judgment in any place, and it will not give any apology, it will not give any symbol, for none of the virtues of the archons, none of the virtues of the emanations of the light may approach this soul; but all the places of the archons, and all the places of the emanations of the light, each of them will sing a hymn in their place, filled with fear in the presence of the light of the jet which clothes this soul until it has crossed them all, until it has gone to the place of the inheritance of the mystery that it has received; and it is the mystery of this unique and ineffable being that is united with its members.

Papus

CLARIFICATION ON THE RECEIVERS

And here is how the angels of light visit the brothers of good conduct, as is revealed a multitude of times on the part of the Lord. If it is a good man who is gone to sleep, three angels come to him according to the degree of conduct of the one who is gone to sleep. If he is elevated in his actions, they send him likewise elevated and glorious angels in order to lead him to God; if he is lacking in his virtues, they send him likewise inferior angels... At the moment when the man is upon the point of rendering his soul, one of the angels stands at his head, another at his feet, under the form of men who anoint with oil from their own hands, until the soul comes out of the body; the other deploys a great spiritual vestiture to clothe it with glory.

If it is the soul of a holy man, we find it beautiful of form and white as snow. And when the soul has come out of the body into the vestiture, one of the angels takes the two ends of the vestiture from behind, and the other from the front, as for a body that men remove from the ground; and the other angel sings before it in a tongue that no one knows, not even those who saw this vision, who are our father Pakôme and Theodore; for they do not know what the angels sang, they only heard the angels singing and saying *alleluia*. It is thus that they walk with the soul, in the air, towards the East, walking not in the manner of men, who walk with their feet; but gliding in their walk like the water which flows, because they are spirits. They walk with the soul towards the heights, so that it sees the limits of the earth inhabited from one end to the other, that it sees all creation, and that it renders glory to God who created it. After this, they show it the place of its repose, according to the order of the Lord, so that after it will have gone into the place of its repose because of the good works that it has done, it knows also the chastisements from which it has been saved, and it blessed even more the Lord who has saved it from all these sufferings by the goodness of Our Lord Jesus Christ[12].

IV

JESUS AND INITIATION

> Where, then, O Egypt, where are the diviners and the horoscopes and those who do not enchant the earth and those who enchant by their entrails? Let them teach you of that hour that the Lord Sabaoth will do his works!
> (Isaiah, 19:12)

Therefore, *the virtue* which was in Isaiah the prophet has prophesied thus before your coming, and it has prophesied to your subject that you will lift the virtue from the archons, from the Aeons, that you will change their Sphere and their Destiny so that they henceforth know nothing. That is why it has said: You know not at all what the Lord Sabaoth will do, that is to say: None among the archons knows what you will do to them from this hour, that is to say of Egypt, for they are matter. The virtue, then, which was in the prophet Isaiah, has prophesied to your subject before, saying: "From this hour you will not know what the Lord Sabaoth will do" because of the virtue of light that you have received from the hand of Sabaoth the Good, the one who is in the place of the Right, virtue which, today, forms your physical body. That is why you have told us, O my Lord Jesus: Let the one who has ears to hear, hear! For you know the one whose heart is said to enter into the kingdom of heaven.

CREATION OF CHRISTIANITY
Involution of the celestial principles which come to constitute the terrestrial individualities which are going to create Christianity

Man possesses within himself the principle of his own ascension. Let him reunite, by whatever means, his immortal spirit with the celestial virtue which accompanies him during life in the physical body, and he becomes a *participant* of *the first mystery,* Valentinus will say, *a saint,* Catholicism will say, *a Chrestos* or *Christos,* say the schools of initiation of the elementary degree, *he will no longer be born,* he will participate in Nirvana, say the Orientals and Brahmanic schools. Now, here is hidden a dangerous trap that it is important to point out.

Every evolution supposes one or two involutions; every man who becomes God necessitates a God who has been made man, as the evolution of food in the intestines necessitates the descent of two forces of superior origin: the blood and the nervous force.

It is the fault of this observation of the *current of sacrifice and love* which precedes the harsh path of initiation and the evolution of the human soul, that the naturalist initiations of the Orient have led many of their adapts to believe that "the state of Christ" was a plane of psychic existence that every man may attain, and which does not necessitate the constant effort of the celestial Christ principle, alone capable by its involution of bringing back to him the evolved souls.

Just as the comet, true sanguine globule of the Universe, as said Michel de Figanières, comes at certain periods to give back the life of the superior centers to the solar families, so too *beyond the constant current* of divine involution and evolution of the human souls, is it necessary, in certain epochs, for a great Divine descent followed by a great ascent of souls in order to give to God the occasion to manifest his absolute love while anticipating the time of the total reintegration of humanity.

To not see existence *as celestial individuality* of the Virgin of Light, of the Christ, and of the other principles, is to stop in one's tracks, to take station in this *mental plane* which leads to materialist pantheism, and to close one's eyes on the existence of the *celestial plane* that the virtues of the heart, love and prayer, reach more rapidly than the mental, critical, and reasoning forces.

Having united the celestial love manifested by grace and redemption with the love of man for heaven, manifested by prayer and sacrifice, this is the whole secret of the power of the Christians, illuminated by Christ and called to rule
the entire earth on the day when they will replace the law of violence with the law of tolerance and love[13].

Valentinus is going to describe to us the descent of the celestial principles which come to prepare the salvation of the race by constituting Christianity. This is all a chapter of that *secret history* of the Savior, reserved, in the first centuries, to the most elevated initiations.

INCARNATION OF JESUS

After this it happened then that, by order of the First Mystery, I looked anew down below towards the world of humanity; I found Mary, the one that they called my mother according to the material body. I also spoke to her under the figure of Gabriel, and when she was turned up toward me, I cast into her the *first virtue* that I had received from the hands of Barbelo, that is to say the body that I have carried on high, and instead of the soul, I cast into her *the virtue* that I had received from the hand of the great Sabaoth the Good, the one who exists in the place of the Right[14]. (Pv. 7.)

THE VIRGIN MARY
It is from the *Virgin of Light* that is issued Mary the mother of Jesus.

Thus you, O Mary, you who has taken form in Barbelo according to matter, and you have taken a resemblance with the virgins of light according to the light, you and the other blessed Mary, the darkness has existed because of you, and also from you is come the hylic body that I wear and that I have purified. (p. 60.)

The following extract is going to give us a presentiment of a new and profound mystery.

Jesus lived as a man until the age of twelve years of terrestrial life. It is only at this age that his divine virtue really takes possession of his physical being. The adepts of the schools of naturalist initiation are going to see here the union of the inferior principles and the superior principles of man in order to constitute the Christ. They said that the Gnostic doctor has foreseen, across the ages, the error to avoid in this case; for he takes care to describe with great detail the involution, the descent of each of the celestial principles which are going to be materialized to constitute a terrestrial being.

INCARNATION OF THE SPIRIT OF JESUS

Then Mary spoke, saying: "My Lord, as to the words that your virtue has prophesied through David, namely: Mercy and truth have been encountered, justice and peace have been brought low; the truth has flourished upon the earth, and justice has looked upon the heights of heaven; your virtue has prophesied these fords formerly to your subject.

"When you were small, before the Spirit had descended upon you, while you found yourself in a vineyard with Joseph, the Spirit is descended from the heights, it is come to me in my house, resembling you, and as I did not know it and thought that it was you, it said to me: "Where is Jesus, my brother, so that I may meet him?" And when it had said this to me, I was at a loss, and I thought that it was a phantom to test me; I took it and I attached it to the foot of the bed which was in my house, until I went to find you in the fields, you and Joseph, and that I had found you in the vineyard. Joseph was occupied with setting the vine in the vine-prop. It happened then that, having heard me say this thing to Joseph, you understood the thing, you rejoiced, and you said: "Where is it, that I may see it? No, I will wait for it in this place." And it happened that Joseph having heard you say these words, was in confusion, and we went together, we entered the house, we found the Spirit attached to the bed, and we looked at you with it, we found that it resembled you. And that which was attached to the bed was unbound, it embraced you, it kissed you and you too kissed it, *you became one sole and the same person*.

"This, then, is the thing and its explanation: the mercy is the Spirit which has come from the heights by the first mystery in order to take pity on the human race; he has sent his Spirit to forgive the sins of the entire world, so that men receive the mystery, that they inherit the kingdom of light. The truth, therefore, is the virtue which has dwelled within me, come from Barbelo; it has become your hylic body, and it has been the herald under the place of the truth. Justice is your Spirit which has brought all the mysteries from on high, in order to give them to the human race. Peace, then, is the virtue which has dwelt within your hylic body according to the world, this body which has baptized the human race, in order to render it stranger to sin and to return it to peace with your Spirit, so that they be in peace with the emanations of the light, that is to say in order that justice and peace are brought down. And according to what has been said: The truth has flourished upon the earth, the truth is your hylic body which has pushed within me into the earth of men, which has been the herald under the place of the truth; and again according to what has been said: Justice has flourished outside of heaven, the justice is the virtue which has looked upon heaven, that which will give the mysteries of light to the human race, and men will become just, they will be good, they will inherit the kingdom of light."

THE TWELVE APOSTLES

Just like the soul of the Christ and Mary, the souls of the twelve apostles do not come from the world of the archons, but rather from the celestial plane, as is affirmed to us in the following extracts:

Rejoice then, be in cheerfulness, for when I came to the world from the beginning, I led with my twelve powers just as I have told you from the beginning. I have received them with the hand of the twelve saviors from the Treasury of Light, according to the order of the first mystery. These mysteries, then, I have thrown into the bosom of my mother since my arrival into the world, and they are now in your bodies, (p.8).

"And the twelve virtues of the twelve saviors of the Treasury of Light that I have received from the hands of the twelve gods of the middle, I have thrown them into the sphere of the archons, and the gods of the archons with their servants thought that they were souls of the archons; and the servants led them. I attached them into the body of your mothers, and, when your time had been accomplished, they put you in the world without having within you the souls of the archons."

ROLE OF THE APOSTLES

"Truly, truly, I say to you: I will make you perfect in all the Pleromas, from the mysteries of the inner to the mysteries of the outer, I will fill you with the Spirit, so that they will call you pneumatics, perfect ones of all the Pleromas. Truly, truly, I say to you, I will give you all the mysteries of all the places of my Father and of all the places of the first mystery, *so that the one that introduces you on earth will be introduced into the light form on high, and the one that rejects you on earth is rejected in the kingdom of my Father who is in heaven,*" (p. 32).

Thus, Valentinus, the Gnostic doctor, author of the *Pistis Sophia,* is precise. All the terrestrial manifestations which have presided over the birth of Christianity are *persons* from the celestial plane. It is by a sublime divine involution that the evolution of the souls is made possible. That is the elevated and particular character of Christianity, the origin of its most profound mysteries.

THE TWO VESTURES (p. 9)

The first has within it the entire glory of all the names of all the mysteries and all the emanations of the hierarchies of the ineffable places.

And the second vesture has within it the glory of the names of all the mysteries and all the emanations which exist in the hierarchies of the two places of the first mystery.

And this vesture that we have sent presently is within itself the glory of the name of the mystery of the commander which is the first order of the mystery of the five abysses, and the mystery of the grand ambassador of the ineffable which is the great light, and the mystery of the five *prohegonomenes* which are the five *parastates*.

∴

We have assisted in the birth of a great period.

As always the law is universal, and secondary periods have just come forth.

Indeed, each human life reproduces the two falls and the two paths of salvation possible.

The first fall is that of the soul into the body of flesh; the second, always avoidable, is the total taking of the soul by the passions and its progressive *"stripping."*

The first path of salvation is the recovery of the soul from the attractions of the flesh, by the holiness of the terrestrial life and total charity.

The second path, complementary to this, is the creation of the total being by the fusion of the two sister souls. This is, in the human, the image of the redemption operated by Christ, and this is a very important key to the way, the truth, and the life.

V

The Key of the Salvation of the Incarnate Soul, or the Evangelical Initiation

Man is on earth in order to reunite his ineffable elements with his divine elements, and this can only be done through *initiation* which transforms the hylics into pneumatics.

The soul which has not been initiated must return *into a body which will lead it to the path of initiation*. There are current truths of which we find all the elements even in the lesser schools of the Orient, who believe, moreover, to have attained, by this teaching, the whole truth. There is nothing to this.

If the soul, in order to be saved and to definitively escape from the "stream of generation," is to be initiated, it is proper to declare that Christ has multiplied the paths of this initiation.

Besides the strictly personal initiation based on suffering and sacrifice, Jesus comes, thanks to the Gospel, to unveil multiple paths of ascent adaptable to all the races of human beings. He comes, moreover, to assert that the initiate, the saint (says the historian), the pneumatic, or the apostle has the right to *remit sins* and to directly initiate the souls that he judges susceptible to receiving this grace.

Valentinus reveals to us furthermore the bonds which attach the old and new testament in the course of the clarifications that Jesus gives to his disciples who question him.

It is therefore a little of the *esotericism of the Gospels* that is going to reveal to us the entire portion of the "Pistis Sophia" of which we must now occupy ourselves.

ROLE OF JESUS

This is why I told you formerly: SEEK THAT YOU MAY FIND. I have therefore said to you: You will seek the mysteries of the light, those which purify the body of matter, and they will make you into pure light, extremely pure.

Truly, I tell you, the race of humanity is hylic. I am fatigued, I have led them to all the mysteries of the light in order to purify them, for they are the dregs of all matter of their matter, for otherwise no soul of the entire race of humanity would be saved and could not inherit the kingdom of the light, if I had not brought them the purifying mysteries. For the emanations of the light have no need of mystery, since they are pure; but the human race has need of purification, because all men are of the dregs of matter. That is why I said to you formerly: Those who are well have no need of a doctor, only those who are ill; that is to say those of the light have no need of mysteries, because they are pure lights, but the human race, it has need, because they are of the hylic dregs.

This is why you are to announce to the whole human race, saying:

Do not stop seeking day and night until you have found the purifying mysteries, and say to the race of humanity: Renounce the entire world and all the matter that it contains, for the one who buys and sells in this world, the one who eats and drinks of its matter, who lives in all its successes and all its relations, gathers other matter by its matter, for this world, all that is in it, all its relations are of the most hylic residuum and they interrogate each on their purity.

For, it is for the sinners that I have brought mysteries into the world, in order that I forgive all the sins that they have committed since the beginning.

That is why I told you formerly, *I have not come to initiate the just;* now then, I have brought the mysteries so that the sins may be forgiven all men, and that they be introduced into the kingdom of the light, for the mysteries are the gift of the First Mystery, in order that it takes away the sins and the iniquities from all the sinners.

I HAVE COME TO BRING DIVISION *(Key of Baptism)*

On the subject, then, of the sayings on the remission of sins that you have told us formerly in parable, saying: I have come to throw a fire upon the earth, and what do I wish but that it be ignited? Thus have you clearly defined, in saying: I have a baptism of which it is necessary that I be baptized, and how will I be held back until it is accomplished? You think that I have come to throw peace upon the earth? No, I have come to throw division. For, from now on, five will be in one sole house, three will be divided against two and two against three.

That, my Lord, is what you have said clearly, the words that you have said. *I have come to throw a fire upon the earth, and what do I wish but that it be ignited?*

That is to say, my Lord, that you have brought to the world the mysteries of baptism, and what will please you except that it devours all the sins of the soul, that it purifies them all?

And then you defined it clearly in saying: *I have a baptism into which I must be baptized, and how will I be held back until it is accomplished?* That is to say that you will not remain in the world until the baptisms are accomplished and have purified the perfect souls. And again, the words that you told us formerly: *You think that I have come to throw peace upon the earth; no, I have come to throw a division, for, from now on, five will be in one sole house, three will be divided against two and two against three,* that is to say that the mystery of the baptism that you brought to the world has made a division in the body of the world, because the spirit of pneumatic imitation, the body, and the Destiny, he has separated to one side, and on the soul too, with the virtue, he has separated to the other side, that is to say that three will be against two and two against three[15].

RENDER TO CAESAR
(Key of the Evolution of the Soul)
The four meanings

When, therefore, the Savior had said these things to his disciples, he told them: Do you understand the manner in which I speak?

Mary surged up anew, saying: Yes, my Lord, I understand the manner in which you speak to us and I will comprehend them all. Now then, on the subject of the words that you told us, my spirit makes thereof within me FOUR MEANINGS, and my man of Light pushes me, he is in joy, bubbling up within me, wanting to come out of me and enter into you. Now then, my Lord, listen to what I tell you of these four meanings which have been within me. *(Render to Caesar.)*

1ˢ meaning. - The first meaning which has been within me on the subject of the words that you have said: Now then, the soul gives the apology and the seal of all the archons which are in the place of the king Adamas, and it gives the apology, the honor, and the glory of all their seals and of the hymns of the places of light. On the subject of this saying that you told us before, when they brought you this denarius, you saw that it was silver and bronze, you asked: What is this image? They said: It is that of the king. When you saw that it was mixed with silver and bronze, you said: Give to the king what belongs to the king, and give to God what is to God[16]. That is to say when the soul has received the mystery, it gives apology to all the archons, and in the place of the king Adamas, it gives honor and glory to all those in the place of the light; and the words, namely that *it shined* when you saw that it was silver and bronze, is the type of that in which is the virtue of light, that is to say the chosen silver which is in the spirit of pneumatic imitation, that is to say the hylic bronze. That, my Lord, is the first meaning.

2nd meaning - The second meaning, thus, that you have finished telling us now on the subject of the soul which has received the mysteries, namely: When it has gone to the place of the archons of the path of the middle, then they come out before it in a great fear, greatly, greatly, and the soul gives it the mystery of fear, and it fears before it, and it puts the Destiny in its place, and it puts the spirit of pneumatic imitation in its place, and it gives the apology and the seals to each of the archons who are on the path, and it gives the honor, the glory, and the glorification of the seals and the hymns to all those in the place of the light. On the subject of these words, my Lord, you told us previously by the mouth of Paul, our brother:

Give the census to those who collect the census, give fear to those who are worthy of fear, give tribute to those who collect the tribute, give honor to the one who is worthy of honor, and give glorification to the one who is worthy of glorification, and deliver nothing to anyone against you. That is to say the soul which has received the mysteries gives the apology to all the places. That, my Lord, is the second meaning.

3rd meaning - As to the third meaning, it is on the subject of the words that you told us formerly: The spirit of pneumatic imitation is the enemy of the soul, such that it makes it commit all sins and all passions, and it leads it into torments because of all the sins that it has made it commit; in a word, it is the enemy of the soul in every fashion - on the subject of what you told us formerly, namely: *the enemies of man are his servants,* that is to say the servants of the soul are the spirit of pneumatic imitation and the Destiny, which are the enemies of the soul at all times, which cause it to commit all sins and all iniquities. That, my Lord, is the third meaning.

4th meaning - As to the fourth meaning, it is on the subject of the words that you have told us: When the soul has come out of the body, when it walks in the path with the spirit of pneumatic imitation, if it does not find the mystery of the dissolution of all the bonds and seals, those which attach the spirit of pneumatic imitation, so that it ceases to combat it: if, then, it does not find it, the spirit of pneumatic imitation introduces the soul before the Virgin of Light who is the judge and judges it, that is to say the Virgin of Light tests the soul in order to find whether it has sinned and also to find whether it has with it the mysteries of the light, and she gives it to one of its receivers, and its receiver leads it away, throws it into a body, and it does not escape the changing of the bodies before it has given its last shekel. On the subject of these words, then, my Lord, you told us formerly: Be in agreement with your enemy as long as you are with him on the road, lest your enemy deliver you to the judge, that the judge deliver you to the servant, that the servant throw you in prison and you will not leave there without having given your last farthing. That is why these words have been said clearly: Every soul which comes out of the body which walks in the path with the spirit of pneumatic imitation and which does not find the mystery of dissolving all the seals and all the bonds, so that it detaches the spirit of pneumatic imitation attached to it, alas, this soul which has not received the mystery in the light, which has not found the mystery of dissolving the spirit of pneumatic imitation which is attached to it, if, then, it has not found it, the spirit of pneumatic imitation introduces this soul to the Virgin of Light, and the Virgin of Light, who is judge, delivers this soul into the hands of one of its receivers and the receiver throws it into the sphere of the Aeons; it does not escape the changing of the bodies, and it does not give the last shekel which belongs to it!

That, my Lord, is the fourth meaning.

Papus

THE INITIATE ON EARTH

It is necessary to forgive the initiate who sins, then hangs himself again at each degree of initiation.

Not only forgive him up to the seventh time, but truly, I tell you, forgive him up to seven times a multitude of times; give him at each time the mysteries from the beginning, those which are in the first place since the exterior. Perhaps you will gain the soul of this brother, so that he inherits the kingdom of the light. That is why, when you have questioned me previously by asking: If our brother sins against us, do you wish us to forgive him unto the seventh time? - I have responded to you: *Not only unto the seventh time, but unto seven times seventy times.* Now then, forgive him a multitude of times, give him each time the outer mysteries, those which are in the first place. Truly, I tell you, the one who will examine a single soul and who will save it, in excess of the light that he has in the kingdom of the light, he will also receive a glory for the soul that he will have saved, so that the one who will save a multitude of souls, in addition to the glory that he has in the glory, he will receive a multitude of other glories for the souls that he will have saved.

For it is because of the souls of men of this kind that I have spoken formerly in parable, telling you: IF YOUR BROTHER SINS AGAINST YOU, reprove him between yourselves; if he hears you, you will have gained your brother; if he does not hear you, take with you another (brother); if he still does not hear you, nor this other (brother), lead him to the congregation, if he does not hear these others let him be for us as a transgressor and a scandal.

And the words that I have told you formerly: *Everything will hold fast from two witnesses to three*, indicates that these three mysteries testify against its latter to repent, and truly, I tell you, if this man repents, there is no mystery which forgives him his his sins and receives his repentance, there is not the least means in the world to hear him by some mystery, whatever it be, unless it be by the first mystery of the first mystery and the mysteries of that ineffable; that one alone will receive the repentance of this man and forgive him his sins, for these mysteries are merciful and compassionate, forgiving at all times.

That is because of the men of this sort (the initiates who, by hypocrisy, mock the mysteries after having received them) that I have spoken of to you previously in parable, saying: The house where you will enter, where they receive you, tell them: Peace be with you, and if they are worthy, then your peace will rest upon them; but if they are not worthy of it, then your peace will return upon you.

SAYINGS OF JESUS (*Pertaining to repentance*)

Let the man who humbles himself be happy, for it is him on whom they will have mercy, (p. 33).

The one whose Spirit is intelligent, I do not impede him; but I exhort him all the more to tell the meaning which has incited him, (p. 62).

Whoever will be filled with the Spirit of Light in order to advance and proffer an explanation of what I say, no one will prevent him from speaking, (p. 83).

The place where your heart is, there too will be your treasure, that is to say the place where each will have received the mystery, it will remain there, (p. 104).

It is I, the knowledge of the Pleroma, (p. 119).

The one who believes in a prophet will receive the wages of a prophet, and the one who believes in a righteous one will receive the wages of a righteous one, (p. 119).

I forgive and I will forgive, and it is for this that has been sent to me the first mystery, so that I may forgive the sins of the whole world, (p 129).

And test him yourselves (the candidate of good faith), in order to know of what mystery he is worthy, and give him the one of which he is worthy and *hide nothing from him,* for if you hide it, you will be subject to a great judgment, (p. 139).

Truly, truly I tell you, not only will I reveal all things about which you ask of me, but from now on I will reveal to you other things than what you think to ask me, those which are not shown to the heart of man, those that do not know all the other Gods which are in men, (p.154).

PATH OF INITIATION

Whoever has worries and suffers under his load, come to me and I will relieve you, for my burden is light and my yoke is sweet.

This mystery (that of the ineffable) is yours and that of whoever will listen to you, will renounce the whole world and all the matter which is in it, will renounce all the evil thoughts which are in it, and all the cares of this Aeon.

Whoever will renounce the entire world and all that is in it, who will submit himself to the divinity, this mystery will be easier to him by far than all the mysteries of the kingdom of light.

THEURGY

Now then, O Mary, not only you, but all the men who will accomplish the mystery of the resurrection of the dead, the one who heals from the demons, from suffering, from every sickness, and also the blind, the lame, the mute and the deaf, the one that I have given you previously - the one who will receive a mystery and who will accomplish it, if then he asks for anything, poverty or wealth, weakness or strength, sickness or sound body, as well as all the healings of the body, with the resurrection of the dead, the healing of the lame, of the blind, of the deaf and mute, and every sickness and every suffering, in a word the one who will accomplish this mystery, if he asks for all the things that I have just said, they will be granted to him with care.

As to the mystery of resurrecting the dead, of healing the sick, do not give it to anyone and do not teach it, for this mystery is that of the archons, it and all its names. That is why you are to give it to no one nor teach it until you have confirmed the faith in the entire world, so that when you enter into the towns or countries, when they do not receive you, believe in you, or obey your words, then you will raise the dead there among them, you will heal the lame, the blind, the various illnesses among them, and by these means they will believe in you, they will believe that you preach the God of the Pleroma, and they will add faith to every word coming from you. This is why I have given you this mystery, until you have established the faith firmly in the entire world.

Truly, truly I say to you, you will be first in the kingdom of heaven before all the Invisibles and all the Gods, save the archons which are in the thirteenth Aeon and those which are in the twelfth Aeon, and not only you, but also whoever will perform my mysteries. When he had said this, he told them: Do you understand in what manner I speak to you? Mary began again, saying: Yes, Lord, it is what you told us formerly, namely: The last will be the first and the first will be the last, the first are those that have been created before us, therefore they are the Invisibles; then are those which have been created before humanity, then the Gods and the archons, and the men who will receive the mysteries will be before them in the kingdom of heaven. Jesus said to her: Take heart, Mary.

You told us previously: *The first will be the last* and the last will be the first; that is to say the last, the whole race of men, will be first in the kingdom of light, in the manner of all those who are in the place of the Heights, it will be those who are the first.

THE TOTAL REINTEGRATION
(Reintegration of the Apostles)

Now then, truly, I tell you, when the number of the perfect are complete, and the Pleroma increases, I will be seated in the Treasury of the Light, and you too will be seated upon the twelve virtues of light until you have re-established all the hierarchies of the twelve Saviors into the place of inheritance for each of them. When he had said these things, he said: Do you understand what I say? Mary then got up and said: Lord, on this subject you have told us before in a parable: You have endured with me in the temptations, I will establish you a kingdom as my Father has established for me, so that you eat and drink at my table in my kingdom, and you will be seated upon twelve thrones to judge the twelve tribes of Israel. He told her: Take heart, Mary.

And in the dissolution of the world, when the Pleroma makes its ascension, when the number of all the perfect souls will have ascended, and when I will be king in the middle of the final Parastasis.

Then all these men who will have received the mystery in this Ineffable will be co-regents with me, they will be seated at my right hand and at my left in my kingdom. And, truly, I tell you, these men are me and I am these men. That is why I told you formerly: *You will be seated at my right hand and at my left in my kingdom and you will reign with me.*

Exegesis of the Soul

VI

TABLES AND KEYS
of the translation of the Pistis Sophia [17]

Repentances of Pistis (one per Aeon)

Psalm

	Psalm	
1st	69th	Mary
2nd	71st	Peter
3rd	70th	Martha
4th	102nd	John
5th	88th	Philip
6th	130th	Andrew
7th	25th	Thomas
8th	...	Matthew
9th	35th	James
10th	120th	Peter
11th	52nd	Salome
12th	109th	Andrew
13th	51st	Martha

Interrogations

The 24 Invisibles, pp. 95 to 97: Mary.
Place of the Initiates in heaven, p. 97: Mary Magdalene.
The Parastases, p. 103: Mary.
Ascension of the souls already in heaven, p. 105: John.
The Mystery of the Ineffable, pp. 1-2: Mary Magdalene.
Do those who die before knowing the word deserve the kingdom? p. 119: Mary Magdalene.
Degree of imitation and degree of brightness, p. 119: Mary Magdalene.
The 12 Mysteries and the unique Mystery, p. 121: Mary Magdalene.
A year of the light has endured in proportion to the years of the world, p. 124, 3,650,000: Mary Magdalene.
How will men cross all the firmaments? p. 126: Andrew.
Evolution of the soul of the righteous, p. 135: Mary.
On repentant sinners, p. 136: John.
On the initiated and non-repentant sinner, p. 137: John.
Individuals having been made to initiate by hypocrisy, p. 140: John.
Intercession of the good for the sinner, p. 142: Mary.
Action of the mysteries announced by Jesus on the destiny of men, p. 143: Mary.
Action of the mysteries on poverty, weakness, sickness. - Gift of the miracle, p. 144: Mary.
What forces man to sin, p. 145: Mary.

Jesus examines successively the evolution of the soul of the one who has always sinned, p. 147: Jesus.

Jesus examines successively the evolution of the soul of the one who has resisted to his best his passions and who has received the movements of initiation, p. 148: Jesus.

Jeus examines successively the evolution of the soul of the one who, after having received initiation, has sinned again, p. 149: Jesus.

Mary gives the four meanings of this evolution by supporting his examples with citations from the Gospels, p. 151: Mary.

On Baptism, p. 164 Mary.

Exegesis of the Soul

ALPHABETICAL TABLE
OF THE Pistis Sophia

Adamas, great Tyrant of all the Tyrants who are in the Aeons	013
Adamas	187
Akhthambas, the unmerciful ones	005
Angels (generation of)	187
Angels (the transgressors have taught magic)	016
Antithesis, Opposition (Binary)	108
Arrogant, one of the three Tridynomos	023
Arrogant, emanation	025
Ascension	003
Avarice	131
Baptism, prevents souls from passing through the chaos	154
Barbelo	007
Blasphemers (chastisement)	200
Body, hylic	015
Books of Ieou	126
Caresses (bad)	131
Ceremony (remission of sins)	196
Chaos, unknown to the souls of the initiates	149-150
Cohabitation (waters of the fall)	187
Credulity	131
Curses (the man who), chastisement	197
David (Ps. VII), key	089
David (Ps. LXVIII), key (1st Rep. of Pistis)	028
David (Ps. LXX), key (2nd Rep. of Pistis)	031
David	084
Death, detailed study	147
Dissolution of the seal (mystery)	148-149
Extreme Unction (key of)	122
Fall	186-187
False witness	131
Forgiveness; Supreme Forgiveness by the ineffable	141
Gabriel (angel)	007
Gabriel	066
God, It is a God who has found the words of the mysteries of the second place of the middle	130
Gods (real meaning)	154
Gods (tyrants)	041
Hell	147
Hierarchy of the archons of the sphere	187
Iabraoth	187
Ialdabaoth, Matter of Pistis thrown into the chaos	025
Ialdabaoth	132

Iao the great	100
Ieou, the guardian of the Light	014
Ieou, guardian of the Light	049
Ieou, the father of my father	???
Ineffable, the	108
Ineffables (supreme forgiveness)	141
Influences, astral (works of)	021
Invisibles (the twenty-four) each is nine times greater than the twelve Aeons together	095
Jesus, his kingdom and his poor	118
Jesus, his power and his kingdom	106
Jesus is the first mystery which *looks outside*; his father is the first Mystery which *looks within*	072
Jesus the merciful is gentle of heart	005
John the Baptist; But it happened that, when I was called by the middle of the archons and Aeons, I will look down on the world of humanity by order of the first mystery; I found Elizabeth, the mother of John the Baptist, before she was conceived, I cast into her a virtue that I have received from the hand of the lesser Iao the good, the one who is in the middle, so that he can preach before me and prepare my way, that he baptize in the water for the remission of sins; it is therefore this virtue which is in the body of John. And furthermore, instead of the soul of the archons that he was obliged to receive, I found the soul of Elijah the prophet in the Aeons of the sphere, I made it enter and I took his soul too, I brought it to the Virgin of Light and she brought it to the receivers; they will lead it to the sphere of the archons and they will cast it into the womb of Elizabeth. It is therefore the virtue of the lesser Iao, the one of the middle, and the soul of Elijah the prophet which are attached in the body of John the Baptist (Elijah)	007
John; John the virgin who will command in the kingdom of light	036
John himself	118
Lance which pierces the side	195
(says John)	187
Last (the), will be first	051
Light (astral)	003
Light (aotral)	004
Light (astral)	193
Light; Effect of the vesture of light, progression of 49 times of the light	011-012
Magic	013
Magic of the archons of the Aeons	015
Magic; and likewise Incantations, whether they invoke the name of the archons, or meet them looking to the left, all that they ask have their *dicans*, they say them with certitude	010
Man (constitution: body, spiritual imitation, soul)	022
Man of light; My man of light has ears, said Mary	028
Mary; Mary the Blessed, you who will make me perfect in all the	

Exegesis of the Soul

mysteries of the inhabitants of On High, speak freely, O you whose heart is right in the kingdom of heaven, more than all the brethren. It is you who will be the Pleroma of all the pleromas, and the Perfection of the perfections	015
Mary Magdalene (her superiority)	118
Melchizedek, the great receiver of light	019
Melchizedek	099
Melchizedek	151
Michael	066
Moses, by two or three witnesses everything will remain. Key: the three witnesses are Philip, Thomas, and Matthew	038
Murderer (chastisement)	198
Murmuring	131
Mysteries (the twelve), gifts that they bring	121
Mysteries (complete): mystery of the 12th Aeon of the archons, their *seals*, their *characters*, the manner to invoke in order to enter into their places; the mystery of the 13th Aeon; mystery of the Baptism of one of the Middle, seal and character; baptism of those on the right, great mystery of the Treasury of the Light	088
Mythology (connections)	187
Odes of Solomon	078
Parable (Samaritan): Give to drink	194
Parables: Starting from this day, indeed, I will speak to you with frankness, from the beginning of the truth unto its perfection, and I will speak to you face to face, without parable	005
Pederasty, chastisement (Dissolution)	207
Philip wrote under the discourses that Jesus said: Listen, Philip the Blessed, to what I speak to you, for it is you, with Thomas and Matthew, that I have charged, in the first mystery, to write everything that I say, every word that I will make, and everything that we will do	037-038
Pistis Sophia	023
Prayer of Jesus	185-186
Pride, boasting	131
Prideful (chastisement)	199
Psalm 95, key	073
Receivers: receivers of light, pacific receivers, and receivers of darkness (analogy with the angels) summary	019
Receivers (pacific) detaching every soul which comes out of the body	116
Reincarnation (summary)	007
Sabaoth the Good exists in the *place of Right*	007
Sabaoth emanates from Ieou	099
Sabaoth	187
Sabaoth the Good is in the *place of Right*	187
Savior; It is a savior and an Infinity, the one who has found the words of the mysteries and the words of the third place, which is in the exterior	130
Scripture (Elijah will come to prepare the way of Christ) key	007

Scripture; Where, then, O Egypt, are the soothsayers and the horoscopes (Isaiah 19:12); changing of the direction given by Jesus in the sphere	014
Sentence, apology, symbol, key of evolution	117
Sentence, apology, symbol, character, seal	126
Sins (various); hardness, evil words, anger, malediction, avarice, katalalia, fighting, ignorance, villainy, outburst, adultery, murder, impurity, atheism, magical preparations, blaspheme, deceitful teachings	132
Sins (seals)	155
Sins (those who forgive them), their names	195
Slander	131
Slanderer (chastisement)	191
Solomon	039
Solomon (Odes)	068
Solomon	081
Souls, Reincarnation	005
Soul (of the hylics) For every man who is in the world has received a soul from the archons of the Aeons	006
Soul; Summary of evolution (rewards)	007
Soul; Jesus has advanced their evolution	118
Souls of men and animals	019
Souls; human, evolved by Jesus	021
Souls; All the human souls which will have received the mystery of the light will precede ALL	107
Soul, coming out of the body	116
Soul. Evolution by death	121
Soul (of the righteous), come out of the body	135
Soul (evolution); It is not possible to introduce a soul into the light Without the mystery of the kingdom of the light	136
Soul; Involution	145
Soul, of the initiate of the first degree	148
Soul; sinner sealed by one's sins by the spirit of imitation	155
Soul (coming out)	196
Souls (dissolution)	199
Sphere of the Aeons is the sphere of the changings	153
Spirit (æsthetic)	033
Spirit of imitation	145-146
Spirit of imitation, attached to the soul by the archons	148
Thieving (chastisement)	197
Trembling of the earth following the ascension of Jesus	004
Two, vestures of glory	009
Virgin of Light	007
Virgin of Light	122
Virgins (the seven) of the Light	150
Virtues: Be: loving the good men, pacific, merciful, compassionate; serve the poor, the sick, those who are pressured; be pious;	

renounce all	135
Zodiac	100-101

Papus

VII

GENERAL CONCLUSION

Connections with occultism – The three stages of psychic evolution – Sectarianism and unity

The reader has just been given an idea of the very curious system exposéd by Valentinus. A commentary has seemed necessary to us to guide the seekers in the reading of the *Pistis Sophia;* we now endeavor to attach these various mysteries to the teachings of occultism.

Being given the very subject of the Gnostic work, it is above all the spiritual plane and only the most elevated part of the astral plane which will make up the matter somewhat expounded upon.

Thus, the Spirit of spiritual imitation is indeed the astral body of the occultists, but this astral body considered solely in its psychical influences.

The Sphinx symbolized, by three animals: ox, lion, and eagle, governed by the human head, the three circles of interior attraction: the instinct, the passion, and the unregulated imagination, opposed to the will and governed by it. Now, these three circles of attraction towards the lower constitute the domain of the Spirit of spiritual imitation, whereas the celestial Virtue presides over the direction of the spiritual consciousness.

On these points, the revelations brought by Valentinus are not as interesting as the wholly new developments that he gives to the question of the agents charged with presiding over the terrestrial birth and death, and that he calls the Receivers, which are themselves qualified according to their ray of action.

We may assert without fear that these notions on the spiritual beings touched upon the most profound mysteries of the temples of initiation of antiquity, and if we know that the Virgin of Light, the celestial Father (IAO), and the Grand Receiver Melchizedek are teachings reserved to the high Kabbalah, we get a clear idea of the light brought into the outer darkness by the Gnostic doctor.

But it does not suffice him to describe to us the various routes which are offered to the soul after death, he insists further, and often, on the truly divine role of the Virgin of Light which offers to the sinful souls salvation through reintegration. The key of the mysteries of birth is thus given, from the second century of our era, at the same time as the key of the mysteries of death.

The Roman Church which has made every effort to misrepresent and to ridicule the teachings of the Gnostics, has, however, never dared to condemn reincarnation, as Dr. Rozier has victoriously demonstrated to us at last *(Initiation,* 1989). It is but a question here of a fact that direct experience permits to the initiated to verify experientially.

∴

But let us leave here these considerations, and let us insist a little upon the evangelical revelation.

What strikes us first of all is the direct link established between the two Testaments by the connections of the Psalms with the Gospel.

Then, we see Jesus appear, such as he was conceived by the initiates capable of realizing his truly divine origin, and capable of knowing that the Son of God is involved and not evolved. "Jesus is the first mystery *which looks outside,* his Father is the first mystery *which looks within."*

So, it seems very useful to us to stop here for a moment and ask ourselves why the occidental occultists have always been truly and profoundly Christians, all while carefully removing themselves from the clerical influences which often replace the domain of Jesus with that of Caesar. The occultists want to be tolerant, even for the clergy who attack them and who slander them, and they would shed the light even into the darkness which represses them. They would seek to enlighten and illumine the souls, but without obliging them to become occultists more than something else, for the truth, like God, is everywhere, and it suffices to dissolve the husks to make it appear.

A Brahmin, staying with the savages who prophesied by the serpents, did not tell these savages to kill the serpents and to convert to Brahmanism, he showed them, on the contrary, how it is necessary to work in order to develop to the maximum the gift of prophecy from the serpent; then he removed himself, sure that the universal Spirit would eventually lead the savages to the path of Unity. Thus acts the initiate of all religions. He goes into the middle of the clergy, into the middle of the sectarians of materialism, and into the middle of the profane, and he enlightens them by leading them to the door of truth that each of their customary paths contains. But he guards himself well from converting them by ruse or by force or by gifts to a particular sect, for it is the very Spirit of Christ, in permanent action upon the earth, which will lead the souls back into the Light, and this without severity and without violence.

It must not, indeed, be forgotten that there are three stages of psychic development in each section of studies, and the occultist is submitted to this rule like all the other seekers until he has penetrated into the place of the Unity - by the spiritual path.

The first stage, obligatory for all when we follow the intellectual path, is the rationalist stage. *The facts* alone strike the spirit without making it uneasy concerning the laws and principles, whether magnetic, spiritist, or magical, it matters little; it is indispensible for seating the reason upon the rock of experience. Here is found the key of the physical sciences through elementary Kabbalah and the rudiments of alchemy.

Many beginners imagine that all of occultism is concluded here, and it is, indeed, here that is found contained all that may be useful to the propagation and diffusion of the elements of the occult.

Thus, the Societies of teaching and commencement, such as the Groupe independant d'etudes esoteriques [Independent Group of Esoteric Studies] and the 1st degree of the *Faculty of Hermetic Sciences* are constituted to lead the student to this stage and to allow him to handle the key of the arts and sciences of the physical plane.

Freemasonry, starting from the Scottish 18°, was also, originally, intended to work along this same path, but today it has degenerated and does not even reach the first stage.

A most curious thing: human intelligence, reaching this point only after having created its autonomy, and after having rid itself of the purely mystical teachings, without experiential basis, imagines itself to have reached the apogee of its development, whereas it is only in its infancy.

Thus, those who claim to be free spirits, liberated from prejudice and superstition, look with a profound disdain upon the brothers who have reached the superior degrees, and who appear to them to have degenerated and regressed. This is a most singular error of the intellect, and even more widespread than one imagines.

For as much as intellectual perseverance and courage have been necessary to sweep away all preconceptions and to admit the occult fact with its consequences, so too is it necessary to come out of the egotism of this first stage and to begin developing the heart and the sentiment, whereas only the cerebral development was necessary in the first stage.

How does one take up the reading of the *Imitation,* of the *Gospel,* or the books of Buddhist morals, how does one attain to the certitude that it is a question here of facts as positive as the occult facts, how, finally, does one open his moral being to prayer and to the influences from on high, when one believes himself *someone,* when he makes himself the *center* of the Universe?

There is for this but a single path of humility and the return to the plane of universal communion where the stone, the planet, and all the modalities of the Soul of the World are united in one same and total thanksgiving. Stop believing yourself somebody; have the sentiment that, before the Immense Power from On High, you are scarcely anything, *fraternize with the lessers who suffer,* go to the poor of heart, spirit, or body, and teach them to bless their trials and to hate no longer, and slowly, your free reason, your prideful will, will bend with success without losing their qualities, and the life of the heart will awaken within us.

Then, the facts will vanish before the *idea* that they reveal and that they convey, the divisions of the religions and sects disappear in the universal love of the sinners and the weak, and the soul, intoxicated by ecstasy and Infinity, flees little by little these terrestrial foundations upon which its activity is to be exercised.

The illuminatus becomes a solitary, a mystic; this is the way of Swedenborg and Louis-Claude de Saint-Martin; it is the path indicated by the spiritualist knighthoods, of which *Martinism* is an example.

But the human being is only complete by the union of the sister-souls, separated during the physical incarnation; likewise, the spiritual Being is born in man in all its splendor only if, by a new and more considerable effort, the man realizes the union of the brain with the heart, of the Fact and the Law in order to develop the unity of the principle.

This knowledge illuminated by faith, this faith coagulated by knowledge, must be dedicated to the evolution of the weak and oppressed, and the action, spiritual even more than natural, ought now be the aim of the one who aspires to the conscious sufferings of the 3rd stage.

Ever unknown, he is to save those very ones who scoff at him and insult him; he is to steer them clear of suffering and to take it on himself in case of need. And never is he to presume the right to make his real powers shown; he cannot say that he is superior to the most ignorant or most sinful of men, for he is in the plane where all superiority has disappeared before the necessity of universal self-sacrifice.

This is the path indicated in the Rose-Croix Illuminati orders; it is the path of the Pneumatic and it is the way that Jesus reveals to those who wish to follow it. One never reaches the *path of the masters of life and suffering* by the astral body; the spiritual body alone is capable of attaining it.

But the student who scarcely approaches the first of these three stages ought to have enough knowledge to respect the mystic, and enough courage to be ready to kill the warrior who combats in his heart for egotism and pride.

Re-read the repentances of *Pistis Sophia,* this permanent model of every being who wishes to unite the devotion of the heart with the knowledge of the brain, seek the divine words, even related by a Gnostic doctor, flee clerical despotism, whether it emanates from the materialist scholar, that clerical of nothingness, or from some sectarian who wishes to convert by strictness, excommunication, or force. And to those who would accuse us of being demoniacal, or of being alienated according to the schools, respond by these eternal words: "Happy is the man who is humble, for it is him upon whom they will have mercy."

Exegesis of the Soul

NOTES

1. In the two Gnostic treatises from Oxford that I have published in the *Notices et Extraite des manuscrits,* v. XXIX, Jesus is exactly in the same role; in the third treatise, known up to the present, that is to say in the adjuration of the papyrus published by Mr. Rossi of Turin, it is very probable that this adjuration is taught by Jesus to his disciples, for the preliminaries strongly resemble the mysteries that we find here and in one of the two Oxford treatises.

2. They correspond to the twenty-four elders of the *Apocalypse,* and have for their key the twenty-four florets which adorn the mystical name of Iod-He-Vav-He. See, on this subject, the works of Eliphas Levi.

3. The notion of the Aeons in the *Pistis Sophia* is applied uniquely to an astral or median plane, and it is, in our opinion, in error that Mr. Amélineau, in his marvelous and so clear introduction, confuses the mysteries applicable to the celestial plane with the Aeons applicable solely to the astral plane.

4. The term *archon* designates all the officials, all the chiefs of the astral cohorts and are differentiated by the function that the archon fulfills. (See the reference to this word in the dictionary.)

5. Theology has represented those two principles, the spirit of imitation by the Angel of Darkness, and the celestial virtue by the Guardian Angel which assists every man in this world.

6. Louis Michele de Figanières has very luminously developed this mystery of the various localizations of the food of man. See especially his study on man's digestion, in the *clef de la vie* (Chamuel, general agent).

7. We find here the origin of a most curious theory, according to which a part of the divinity of the fallen angels (that the archons represent here exactly) would have served as the foundations of the divine principles of the human soul. This theory deserves very serious study.

8. It is useful to follow the various phases of this evolution on the grand general table.

9. Follow its phases on the grand general table.

10. I have suppressed a repetition which would obscure the text.

11. Thirteenth Aeon.

12. E. Amélineau, *Monum. pour servir à l'hist. de l'Ég. Chrét.,* II, life of Pakôme, p. 121-123.

13. See on this subject the beautiful articles by *Amo* in *l'Initiation* and other spiritualist journals.

14. Thus contrary to the customary constitution of human beings, all the principles owing to the constitution of the personality of Christ come from the celestial plane. In the ordinary man, the celestial virtue alone (which is not incarnate) comes from this plane.

15. See the constitution of the human being in chapter 3 of this book.

16. See Matth., XXII, 21; Mark XII, 17; Luke XX, 25.

17. All the pages indicated below are those of the translation of Mr. Amélineau. You are asked to refer there.

Exegesis of the Soul

LIBRARY OF OCCULTIST PROPAGANDA
Published under the direction of the Martinist Order

HOW IS THE HUMAN BEING CONSTITUTED?

The Body - The Astral - The Spirit and their correspondences

The Human Auras - Key of the Constitutions in nine, seven, and five elements

by
The Doctor PAPUS
Director of the Free Higher School of the Hermetic Sciences
Officer of Public Instruction

Small summary, entirely unpublished,
with 3 tables and 20 figures

PARIS
EDITION DE L'INITIATION
CHAMUEL, PUBLISHER
1900

Exegesis of the Soul

Primordial Question

How is the human being constituted? Is it only the body which produces all its faculties?

Has it an immortal soul, or a Spirit united to this body?

If the body and the Spirit exist in man, are they independent of one another, or are they united by another element?

Such are the problems which the philosophers have debated for many ages, and it is to these problems that we now give a solution by exposing the teachings of the occult and Christian tradition of the Occident.

In this little exposé, intended for all, we will give as little philosophy as possible, and we will not establish any debate. Those who wish to verify our assertions are asked to refer themselves to the great works of the masters and to the complete studies on occultism.

Let us look first of all at the three fundamental questions.

1.   Does the human being have only a body which produces all its faculties?

We answer NO to this question in basing ourselves over all on the following few facts:

A - In less than five years, all the cells of the body have disappeared and have been entirely replaced without the body having changed form and without the look of the person having been disturbed. The material cells are only the instrument, modeled by a power other than matter.

B - Claude Bernard has demonstrated that each of our ideas necessitates the death of the nerve cell which has served in support of it. When we remember an event that happened ten years prior, more than a million different nerve cells have carried the stereotype of the idea which is therefore independent of these cells and their transformation.

C - The phenomena of transcendent hypnotism, the communication from brain to brain without intermediary material, the appearance of the image of one living in danger of death to one's parents at very great distances, the action at a distance and without material intermediary of the nervous force and of the Thought of the human being, and a multitude of deeds of the same kind, shows outside of every philosophical system that the body is not the sole element which constitutes us.

2.   Is the Human Being constituted by a mortal body and an immortal Spirit, without another Principle?

To this dogmatic assertion of certain theologians and of many philosophers, we respond again, NO; in invoking the following principal reasons:

A - Anatomy shows us in man two distinct nervous systems, each served by a type of muscles. First, the conscious nervous system, served by the striated muscles; then the unconscious nervous system of organic life, served by muscles with smooth fibers.

B - Physiology shows us that, during ordinary sleep, the conscious system ceases all its functions, whereas the ganglionary nervous system pursues and operates all on its own. This duality of the systems ought to imply the duality of the constitutive principles.

C - Every tradition, Egyptian, Kabbalistic, Gnostic, Hermetic, corroborated by Saint Paul, asserts the existence of an intermediary principle between the mortal body and the immortal Spirit; a Principle called by Saint Paul *anima*, in his distinction *corpus, anima,* and *spiritus.*

A multitude of experiments of occultism prove the possibility of projecting this intermediary principle outside of the body, during life.

Schema of the three centers of the physical body (Abdomen, Chest, Head) arranged upon the vertebral column.

3. Man is therefore composed of Three Principles:
   1. The physical and material body.
   2. An intermediary principle.
   3. The immortal Spirit.

Such is the question to which we respond YES, just as have done the Egyptians since the 15th century before our era, as well as all the schools of initiation and prophecy which have transmitted the Kabbalah, Gnosis, Alchemy, and the Occult Sciences under all their forms, as have asserted Socrates, Plato, and all the Neoplatonists, and as asserts Saint Paul.

It is to the rapid demonstration of this question that we dedicate this small work.

The Three Principles

The first peril to avoid is the system *a priori* which has for itself the assertion of one author. If man is really constituted by three great Principles and not by five, nor by six, nor by seven, nor by nine, nor by twenty-two, nor by any of the other multiple divisions established by subsidiary analyses, the whole physical constitution of the human being ought to show us, *to cry out to us,* this law of the Trinity. For nature does not change its laws according to the planes, and each piece of the Human Being must repeat the greater general law.

How many parts has the digit of a hand? Three (phalanx, middle section, and ungual phalanx).

How many parts has my upper limb? Three (hand, forearm, arm). How many parts has my abdominal limb? Three (foot, leg, thigh).

How many parts, finally, has my body considered besides the limbs? Three (the abdomen, the chest, the head).

And these are not artificial divisions, for special bones or very particular organs exist for each of these three great segments.

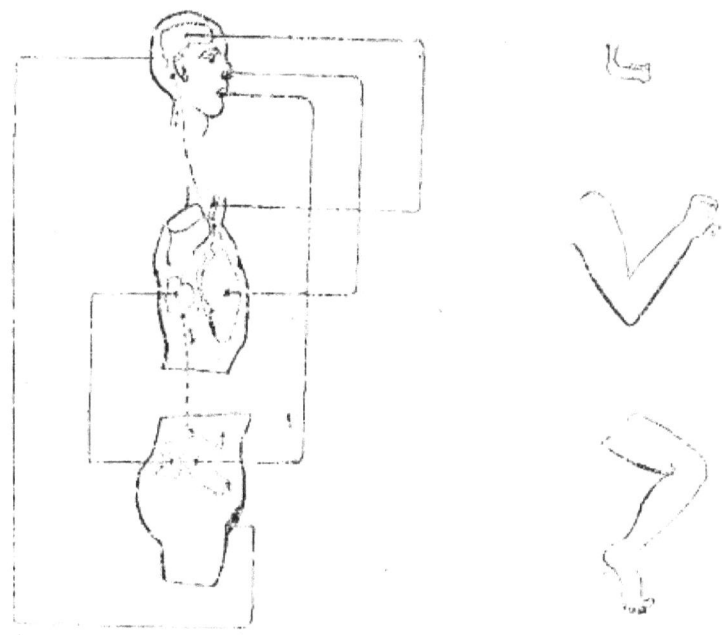

THE TRINITY IN THE PHYSICAL BEING
The three sections (Abdomen, Chest, Head) of the physical Being and the members corresponding to each section. - Organic connections
of the sections between themselves and with the face.

But if the number Three is repeated to infinity in the physical body, other numbers appear. Thus we have two times five fingers, and we have seven openings in the head. (Two eyes, two ears, two nostrils, one mouth.)

This indicates to us that we are not to be dogmatics or sectarians, and that we have to seek the raison d'être of all these accessory numbers, having for their aim to develop in us certain aspects and certain sub-divisions of the great constitutive Trinity.

In order to avoid any obscurity, let us request of the physical body the key of all your deductions. It is analogy, the characteristic method of occultism, which will aid powerfully the deduction and induction.

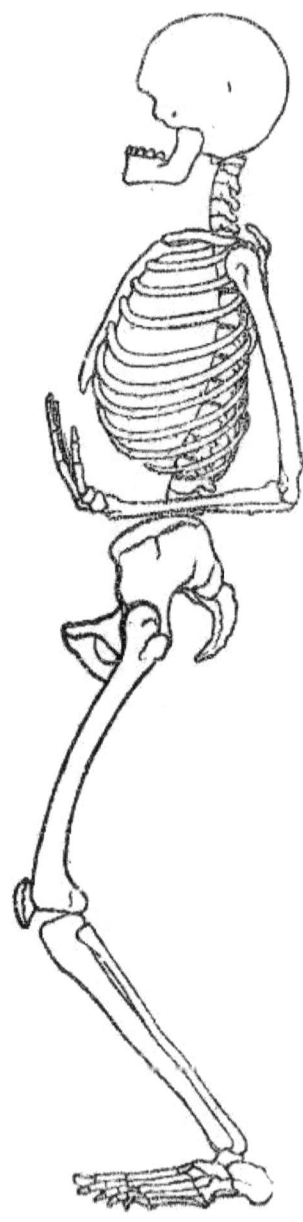

The three centers of the Physical Body and the three pairs of Limbs (abdominal, thoracic, and cephalic), triply divided.

Exegesis of the Soul

THE PHYSICAL BODY - THE ASTRAL BODY
The Animal-Man and the Spirit-Man

The human body presents to us three great centers, the abdomen, the chest, the head, to each of which are attached a pair of limbs.

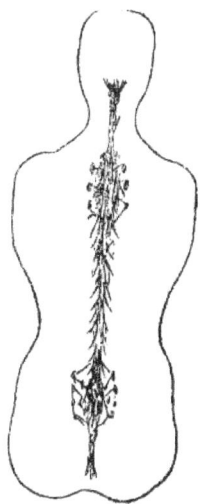

The three large plexuses of the grand sympathetic
Cervical Plexus, Cardiac Plexus, Solar Plexus
Organic centers of action of the Astral Body.

To the abdomen are attached the abdominal limbs (thigh, leg, foot); to the chest, the thoracic limbs (arm, fore-arm, hand); to the head, the cephalic limbs (lower jaw).

Each of these centers has a well characterized physiological function: the abdomen transforms the food coming from the exterior into human substance or chyle; the chest transforms the chyle into blood; and the head extracts from the blood the nervous force which drives the whole human machine. Furthermore, each of the three great centers is represented in the other two. Thus, the abdomen has its chyliferous and lymphatic ducts throughout the whole human being; the chest sends the blood, activated through respiration, into the other centers too; and finally, the head drives, by its nervous dependencies, all the organs without exception.

What is curious and interesting to us, is that all this organic work of abdominal, thoracic, and cephalic factories is done absolutely outside of the intervention of the consciousness and will of the human being. This is solely the work of the *Animal-Man*, and the *Spirit-Man* has functions and organs to it quite distinct from the previous.

The *Animal-Man* is operated by a special nervous system, the nervous system of vegetative organic life, constituted nearly exclusively by the grand sympathetic nerve, its plexuses, and its dependencies. This is what makes our heart beat, what contracts or dilates all our arteries and all our veins, what makes the liver, the stomach, the intestines, and the lungs to work even without troubling itself to know whether the Spirit-Man is awake or asleep, for all the organs work as well during sleep as when we are awake. This is even what repairs the cells used and replaces them, what eats, by means of the embryonic cells and the white globules, the microbes coming from the exterior, what heals the superficial wounds of the skin, and finally, what occupies itself with the whole organic kitchen. The Spirit- Man has nothing to do with all this. Who is it, then, that directs this whole special nervous system?

THE PHYSICAL ORGANS OF THE ASTRAL MAN
The principal plexuses of the Grand Sympathetic and their radius of action
(Semi-schema)

For, we have seen, a system of organs *is only a support of something*. The organs sustain the function but do not create it since their cells die as the function is accomplished.

This principle which directs all the work of the physical body has received many different names across the ages, for it has been known since the greatest antiquity. The Egyptians called it the Luminous Body (Kha); the Pythagoreans, the Chariot of the Soul; the Latins, the Animating Principle (*Anima*) like Saint Paul; the Hermetic Philosophers designate it under the name of *Plastic Mediator* and *Universal Mercury*; Paracelsus and his school, as well as the disciples of Claude de Saint-Martin, the Unknown Philosopher, have called it the *Astral Body* because it draws its Principle from the interplanetary or astral substance.

Whatever the name one gives it, it is necessary to grasp well that this principle has within our being organs to it, a nervous system to it, functions to it, and that its existence is as certain for the occultist as for the physiologist. We shall call it *Astral Body*.

It is the *hidden worker* of the human being, it is the horse of the organism, of which the physical body is the carriage, and of which the conscious being is the coachman.

The horse is stronger than the coachman, it is that which draws the carriage, and yet it is the coachman, less strong but more intelligent, which directs the horse, and by this, the carriage.

Likewise, in the human Being, the Animal-Man is stronger than the Spirit, it is that which drives the human machine, and yet it is the Spirit-Man, less strong, but more intelligent, which directs, in the exterior life, the Animal-Man, and by this, the entire human machine.

In order to understand this well, let us return to the study of the body.

The body has three centers: the abdomen, the chest, and the head; but by this word head we mean the cranium and its contents, that is to say the *horizontal* part of the upper centers. Before the cranium and *vertically* is placed a series of organs constituting *the face*, and these organs have this peculiarity, that they function, for the most part, while we are awake, that is to say while the Spirit-Man is in operation over the outer (what the philosophers call the *non-ego*).

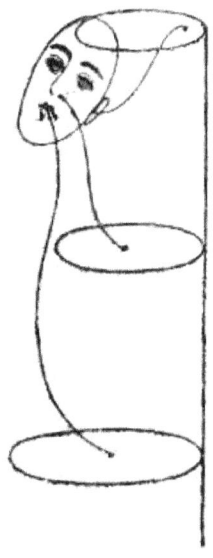

Synthesis of the three Human Centers:
The Mouth, gateway to the abdomen; the Nose, gateway to the chest,
the Ears, gateway to the brain.

When we are asleep is when the eyes are closed, the ears cease their function, the mouth is closed, the sense of smell stops, and only breathing stirs the nostrils. The organs of the face belong therefore to the Spirit-Man and not to the Animal-Man, and each of them has for its aim to establish a control over each of the centers of this Animal-Man.

Thus the mouth (which presents a single opening because the stomach is simple and not double), is the gateway to the abdomen with a faithful doorman which is *the taste* having the charge to allow to enter only the things which please the Spirit-Man. So all that occurs in the abdomen will come to be depicted on the mouth and its appendages (coated tongue from stomach disorders, dry and parched tongue from intestinal inflammations, discolored and dry lips from peritonitis, etc., etc.).

The nostrils have two openings because the pulmonary organs are double; they are the gateway of the chest with a faithful doorman which is *the sense of smell* charged with warning the Spirit-Man of the places where breathing is dangerous for the organism. All that occurs in the chest comes to be depicted on the nostrils or their appendages (fatigued look from cardiac trouble, red cheeks from pneumonia, etc., etc.).

The ears are the gateway of the cephalic nervous system, and the eyes are especially connected to the Spirit-Man. Thus stroke and anemia of the brain are depicted on the ears, whereas madness and psychic troubles are depicted on the pupil and in the sight.

The Spirit-Man is therefore certainly the coachman of the Organism: through the taste and the mouth he presides over the choice of food which is going to be transformed by the abdomen and repair the matter of the whole human being.

THE ANIMAL-MAN AND THE SPIRIT-MAN
All the parts of the figure tinted *in black* indicate the domain
upon which the Will may act; the parts *in white* indicate on the
contrary the domain of organic Life upon which the Will has no
direct force, it is the domain of the Animal Man,
of the inferior Astral Being.

Through the sense of smell, he presides over the choice of the breathable environment, and by the pneumo-gastric nerve over the respiratory rhythm, and therefore over the distribution of the life, heat, and force into the whole organism.

Exegesis of the Soul

Finally, by sight and hearing he presides over the entrance of the sensations already filtered by touch, and by this, over the nourishment of its higher faculties.

Let us end this study of the body by saying that the abdomen is the headquarters of the physical body; the chest is the headquarters of the Astral Body; finally, the head serves as center on the one hand to the intellectual part of the astral body, that we will call psychic being, and on the other hand to the Spirit-Man himself.

Let us occupy ourselves now with the relations of these various principles (physical body, astral body, and Spirit) between themselves.

∴

THE THREE PSYCHIC CENTERS

Plato made the philosophers laugh hard in saying that man had three souls. Now, each of the Principles being represented in all the others (for Nature does not separate its creations by isolated blocks), it follows that there is no reason for each center of man to not have its intellectual manifestation, its ray of spirit more or less obscured, as it has from the chyle, the blood, and the nervous force.

Anatomy already indicates this fact to us in showing us that the spinal marrow expands to the level of the three great centers, with a supplementary expansion for reproduction. But where this fact becomes even more clear, is when we see that the Grand Sympathetic nerve, *which is the true physical support of the astral body*, also presents three great plexuses, the one cervical for the cephalic, another cardiac for the chest, and the other, finally, abdominal (or solar) for the abdomen with an appendage for reproduction.

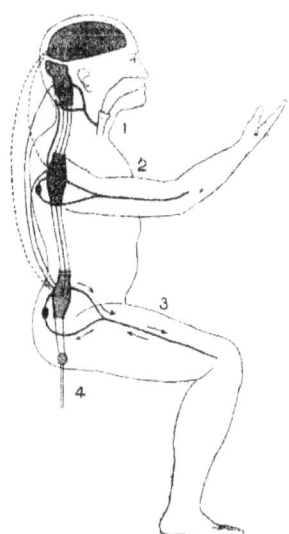

The three medullary expansions and their triple action
upon the Larynx, the Arm, and the Leg.
Semi-Schema extracted from *La Physiologie synthétique*

If we leave the physical domain to address ourselves to the observations, not of the philosophers but of the every-day man, we will ascertain that when a great grief, a great joy, or unexpected news happens to us it is not in the head, but rather in the chest and at the level of the heart that we *receive a blow*, to speak as the people. That is the common reaction of the intelligence of this center.

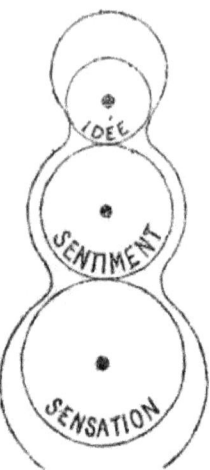

Psychological adaptation of the three Principles of Man.

When, despite the courage commanded by the spirit, a physical reaction is produced, whether at the moment of an exam or upon the field of battle, it is not in the head but in the abdominal center that the sensation is produced, with consequences, well known by the poor soldiers. It is necessary, once again, to decide against the quibbles of the philosophers.

We are thus led to see that Plato had reason, in his account of the secret teachings of the Egyptian Temples, and that just as the body presents three centers, so do three Principles inhabit these three centers; likewise, these three Principles manifest three kinds of intellectual manifestations.

Thus the physical center will manifest *the instinct with the sensation* as means of reaction, and pleasure or pain as results of the movement produced.

The astral center will *manifest the intuition with the sentiment* as means of reaction, and love or hate as results of the emotion produced.

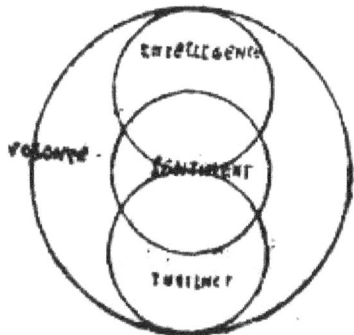

The psychic center will manifest *the idea* with *the intelligence* as means of reaction, and truth or error as results of the impulse produced.

Thus, the world of instincts, that of passions, that of intellectual impulses, the first characterized by wine, the second by women, the third by pastimes, are going to come to deliver assault to the Spirit which rules and governs them (or may govern them) all, as the Mouth governs the abdomen and the Nostrils the lung, in the physical body.

The Spirit, thanks to the will served by the nervous force, may oppose itself to the impulses of the intelligence of the body, which wants to fall asleep by alcohol; to that of the astral which wants to annihilate itself through passion; to that, finally, of the psychic or superior astral being which wants to lose itself in the emotion of games.

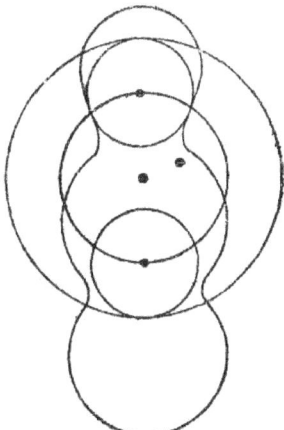

The three impulsive circles and the equilibrating circle of the Will.

But for this it is necessary to accustom the organs which serve the Spirit to their functions as regulators and chiefs, and not to let themselves fall asleep and rust in inaction.

That is why the military schools which seek to spiritualize the centers under the influence of the passions, the ecclesiastical schools which seek to spiritualize the physical being, and the magical schools which tend to develop the will have, each, through suitable exercises and teachings, have the common aim of crushing the lower reaction by putting it into the service of the higher forces.

This teaching is necessary, but it hides a trap: that of making man forget that he is nothing but a weak being, and making him believe that he is something by himself and nearly a God, when his omnipotent Will coming from his domain commands not only his personal organs, but even the visible and invisible forces of Nature.

Just as the fire which comes out of the burning log in the chimney is not created by the matter of the tree, but is only from the sun fixed by this matter and which returns to its center, and as the tree which said that it is he who has made the sun will be mocked by it, so are the forces generated by man only products of refraction come from the divine plane in the final analysis.

Thus, the old alchemists had placed an *oratory* beside each *laboratory* in order to show that Prayer is always the corollary of magic and that humility is the necessary corrective of every spiritual evolution.

The preceding considerations have given a presentiment of the raison d'être of our stay on earth. We are going to attempt to elucidate a little this important problem, in looking at some points of the invisible part of man, or the auras produced by its physical, moral, and intellectual actions.

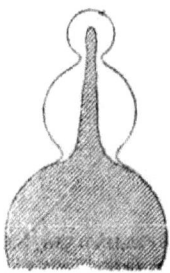

THE PHYSICAL PRINCIPLE
Center. The Abdomen. - Emanation into the Chest and Head.
The *Auras* of the Human Being. - *The Recording of ideas in the Invisible.*

A series of very curious experiments pursued at the outset by an American scientist by the name of Buchanan have come to show that each object may *relate* a part of the events in which it has assisted. The Science which derives from this practice is called *Psychometry* or *Measure* or *Description* by *means of the soul*, for it consists in placing the object to study on the forehead of a human being trained to this end. The soul then sees directly a series of images which are connected to the most important events with which the object has been mingled.

Let us give an example to be better understood. One day in a meeting in which assisted several scholars and men of letters, I had led one of our friends who has developed within him this faculty of Psychometry. An assistant gave him to study an old watch that he carried on him. My friend saw: 1. First a court (style of Louis XIV), nobles, and duels. 2. A scene of the French Revolution in which an old lady rose to the scaffold and was guillotined.

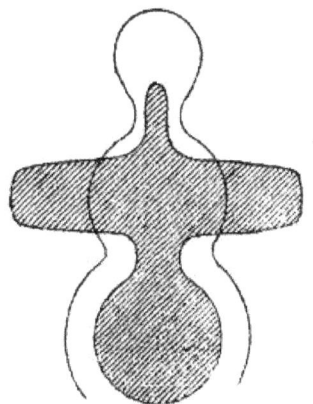

THE ASTRAL PRINCIPLE IN THE HUMAN BEING
Center. The Chest. - *Incarnation* in the Abdomen and the Head.
(Schematic representation)

3. A scene of surgical operation in a modern hospital.

The person who had given the watch was stupefied; this watch had belonged to one of his ancestors killed in a duel under Louis XV; 2. Has a grandmother guillotined under the revolution; 3. Placed in storage, it was taken out and carried the day of an operation performed on the wife of the assistant.

I cite a personal case of Psychometry; but one will find hundreds in the special books.

What results from all these phenomena is that each object may carry its history written *invisibly* around it.

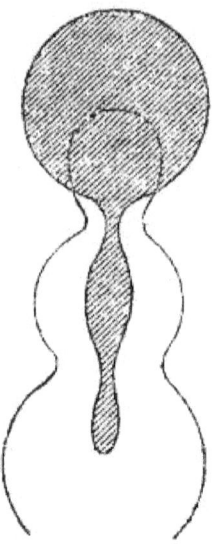

THE SPIRITUAL PRINCIPLE
Its localization in the three centers of Man
(Schematic Representation)
Center: the Head. - Incarnation in the Chest and the Abdomen.

It is the same for the human being. Each of us carries around him a *radiance invisible* to the eye of flesh, but perceptible for the trained soul.

In this radiance are inscribed under the form of images the most important results of our thoughts and actions. This radiance is called, according to tradition, the *auras*, and there is one aura for each Principle. There is, therefore, a radiance or *aura* of the physical body, very little extended; a radiance or *aura* of the astral body; finally, a radiance or *aura* of the Spirit. It is this last which has been known by the religious traditions which have surrounded the heads of saints and divinities with halos in order to symbolize it.

It is thanks to this radiance of the Principles of the Human Being that many phenomena strange in appearance are explained, like the sudden sympathies or antipathies at the time of the first encounter of a being, like the intuitions and previsions called unconscious, etc., etc.

The trained occultist, that is to say who has developed his faculties of perception of the invisible, gets a clear idea at first sight of the real value of a human being, not according to his clothes, not according to his exterior look, but according to his invisible radiance.

Exegesis of the Soul

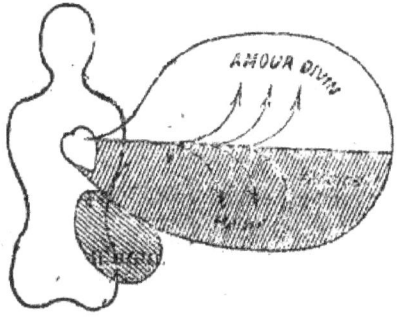

THE ASTRAL AURA
Populated by the sentiments (diagram).

The man who believes himself good, or powerful, or superior to other men, the one who judges and ceaselessly criticizes others, the one who believes to avoid suffering through isolation, instead of sharing that of his fellow beings, all those ones populate their invisible atmosphere with ugly images that the seer and even the sleep-walker from the corner will see perfectly.

By contrast, the good actions, the certainty that one is not better than the others and that the circumstances alone have permitted you not to do the evil that they accuse the others of having done, the humiliations freely consented and supported without weakness, the exercise of true charity, not only physical, but especially moral; all this populates the invisible atmosphere with beautiful sympathetic representations, luminous images that they call in the circles of initiates: *stereotypes*.

Diagram of the Spiritual Aura
The images of the good actions are in the white part, the representations of the evil actions in the black part. - To the left of the white part is Humility, in the middle Charity, to the right is Prayer. - To the right of the black part is Slander, in the middle Pride (the serpent), to the left is Idleness.

The objects, the individuals, the nations, and the stars each have their good or evil stereotypes, and it is to their study that were devoted the ancient colleges of prophets.

∴

We see by this that the human constitution is the true key of the mysteries. The particular study of the astral body will show us how this Principle may come out of the human being, act and appear at a distance, influence beings in good or evil, explaining the majority of the phenomena of Magnetism, Spiritism, and Magic. This study requires a special work which will complete the latter.

Let us just remember in ending that the human being is not composed solely of a body, nor solely of a body and an immortal Spirit, but that in the image of the creative Trinity, it is composed of a body, and astral body, and an immortal Spirit, or to say as Saint Paul, a body, a soul, and a Spirit.

This is the real classification and natural correspondence to the division of the body, to that of its members, to that of all Nature, and to the key of the constitution of the Being given by the three membranes of the Embryo.

VARIOUS CLASSIFICATIONS OF THE PRINCIPLES
Classification in 9, 7, and 5 elements

One may, in proceeding from this natural classification, analyze man in an even more profound manner in noting that each Principle has, itself, three adaptations. Thus the physical body is adapted into three sections in order to support the other Principles (abdomen or support of the physical, thorax or support of the astral, and head or support of the Spirit). The astral body also manifests itself under three modalities according to what it is in relation with the physical body, with its own center, or with the Spirit. the Spirit is polarized under three aspects according as it spiritualizes the physical body, the astral, or as it acts upon its own center.

Head / Nerves	SPIRIT	Psychic Being / Intellectual Life
Chest / Blood	SENTIMENT	Organic Life
Abdomen / Lymph	INSTINCT	Cellular Life

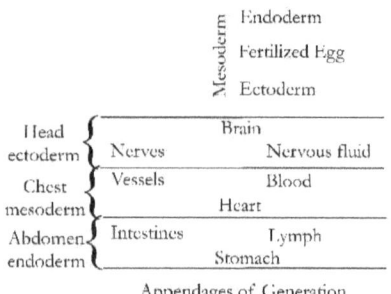

	Creative Principle	
	Creative Principle	
	GOD	
Head	SPIRIT	Psychic Being
Chest	SENTIMENT	Organic Life
Abdomen	INSTINCT	Cellular Life
	GENERATION	
	Reflection of the	
	Creative Principle	
	in Matter	

In order to be clear, we are going to use general terms and avoid all the technical words. We will do away with the falsehoods often presented as truths to the beginners in these studies.

The three Principles constituting man are: the Physical Principle, the Astral Principle, and the Spiritual Principle.

We will call them: Physical, Astral, Spiritual.

These Principles are united to one another. One sole word is necessary for us, it is the word UNION.

We thus obtain in applying to our study the arrangement of the Tarot and of the Sephiroth which alone gives the Occidental Tradition:

For the Physical:
Physical Center.
Union of the Physical and the Astral.
Union of the Physical and the Spiritual.

For the Astral:
Union of the Astral and the Physical.
Astral Center.
Union of the Astral and the Spiritual.

For the Spiritual:
Union of the Spiritual and the Physical.
Union of the Spiritual and the Astral.
Spiritual Center.

This gives us *nine divisions* or nine *Elements*, three of which are primordial Principles, and six derived elements.

Do you wish to name them? Let us rely on the occidental, that is to say the clear and methodical.

Let us ask of the Kabbalah and the Tarot their rigorism and all these elements are going to name themselves with simplicity.

For this, let us cast a glance upon the following table which summarizes what we have just said. The *horizontal* columns indicate the modalities of one same Principle, and the *vertical* columns are the representations of one Principle in the others.

Spiritual Center	Union of the Spiritual and the Astral	Union of the Spiritual and the Physical
Union of the Astral and the Spiritual	Astral Center	Union of the Astral and the Physical
Union of the Physical and the Spiritual	Union of the Physical and the Astral	Physical Center

The first Vertical column will be that of the Spirits.
The second vertical column will be that of the Souls.
The third, that of the bodies.
We have thus:
The Physical or *Physical Body*.
The union of the Astral and the Physical or *Astral Body* (corporeal part of the astral); the union of the Spiritual and the Physical or *Spiritual Body*.

This is the spiritual body of Saint Paul, that Chariot of the Soul of Pythagoras, that element so difficult to comprehend when one has not studied its origin.

Let us look at the souls.

The union of the Physical and the Astral will be the *Physical soul* (the physical part of the soul).

The Astral Center will constitute the *Astral Soul* or real center of the animic principle.

The union of the Spiritual and the Astral will constitute the *Spiritual Soul*.

Likewise would be defined the Physical Spirit (union of the Physical and the Spiritual), the *Animic Spirit* (center of the spiritualization of the soul), and the *Spiritual Spirit* (personal center of the Spirit).

∴

If we consider the human being constituted, we will see that each of the Great Principles acts as an electrical current whose encounter with another current produces a spark. These sparks have been wrongly confused with the principle, for they generally last only some time longer than the terrestrial life.

Moreover, the elements of Union are often confused in such a way that the Union of the Physical and the Astral and that of the Astral and the Physical, for example, constitute one sole element instead of two. It is thus that the Human Being appears under the aspect of *seven elements*, as taught in certain Buddhist sects; of *five elements* as say several Brahmanic schools.

The following small table will allow the reconstitution of these divisions:

Exegesis of the Soul

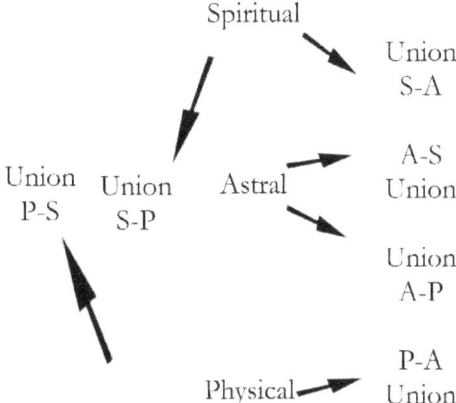

But what any occultist belonging to a serious initiation will not let pass without protesting, is the assertion without proofs that the septenary system is the sole key of the constitution of man, whereas this is in total contradiction to the most elementary anatomy, physiology, and observation.

A septenary is, in general, the point of expansion of a system of which the ternary is the base; and all becomes obscure, diffuse, and incomprehensible, if one does not proceed by the primordial study of the creative ternary.

This is the path followed by Jacob Boehme, the master of the Christian theosophists; this is the path of all those who prefer order and logic to teachings without method and impossible to clearly set forth.

And this is where we fall, in our turn, into obscurity. For many readers will find the last part of our study rather dry. It is only later that they will grasp the full importance.

To try to explain to them how all these terms pass from the three to the nine, then from the nine to the seven, we are going to give a very common example, that of the carriage, the horse, and the coachman; and in following this image, he will get a clear idea of the manner by which one may study the elements constituting man during life. Another work will teach us what all this becomes after death.

THE CARRIAGE TEAM
Analogical image of the Human Constitution
Large numbers: 1. The coachman (director), image of the Spirit.
2. The horse (mover), image of the Astral
3. The carriage (moved), image of the Body.
(The small numbers indicate the sub-divisions.)

An equipage is composed of three constitutive principles: a carriage, a horse, a coachman. The carriage, passive and moved, is the image of the physical body; the horse, passive and mover, is the image of the astral body; and the coachman, active and director, is the image of the spirit.

But the coachman is composed, in his turn, of three parts: the head, the arms, the body. The horse has three parts also: the head, the body, the hooves. The carriage has three parts: the seat, the body of the carriage, the wheels.

There are nine principles which exist when the carriage is in the coach-house, the horse is in the stable, and the coachman is in his room.

But let us reunite these three elements and see what it becomes: the *arms of the coachman* are going to be intimately united with the *head of the horse* in order to constitute, through the reins, the directive system of the equipage.

On the other hand, *the body of the horse* is going to be united with *the body of the carriage* by means of the shafts in order to constitute the driving system of the equipage.

There are nine elements reduced to seven as follows:

Exegesis of the Soul

	Equipage not constituted	Equipage constituted
Coachman	Head of the Coachman 9 Arms of the Coachman 8 Body of the Coachman 7	Head of the coachman 7 Body of the coachman 6 Reins. - System of direction. Union of the arms of the coachman and the head of horse 5
Horse	Head of the horse 6 Body of the horse 5 Hooves of the horse 4	
Carriage	Seat of the carriage 3 Body of the carriage 2 Wheels of the carriage 1	Hooves of the horse 4 Shafts - driving system 3 Seat of the carriage 2 Wheels of the carriage 1

Extract from the *Traité élémentaire de Science occulte* (5th edition), p. 289.

∴

We have already said that the majority of the discussions showed *different names* given to *the same principle* by various philosophers or various schools.

This little summary of the human constitution being above all intended for beginners in these occult studies, we believe to render service to them in summarizing in one table the different names given to each principle by various authors and in various eras, as well as in different Traditions.

This table is very incomplete. It has for its aim only to show the student how it is necessary to seek before all where is placed the principle of which an author speaks. Finally, it is also necessary for the student to accustom himself to bringing back to the ternary, that is to say to the three terms, the enumerations in 5, 7, or 9 principles that he may encounter.

Finally, it must never be forgotten that the intermediary principle, being double in its action, often has two names.

	Material & Inferior Principle	Intermediary Principle	Superior Principle
Contemporary occultism id.	Body Physical Body	Soul Astral Body	Spirit Spirit
Hermetic Philosophers	Body	Plastic Mediator	Spirit
Some Rose-Croix and certain occultists	Body	Life or Spirit	Immortal Soul
Spiritist schools (Allen Kardec)	Body	Perispirit	Spirit
Ancient Egyptians	Khat	Ka and Khon	Bai
Kabbalah	Nephesch (or Gaph)	Ruach (and Imago)	Neschemah
Pythagoreanism	The Flesh	Shadow & Shades	Spirit

Papus

Paracelsus	Elementary Body	Central Fire	Immortal Soul
Hindus	Rupa	Kama Rupa (or linga Sharira)	Atma
Chinese	Xuong	Khi	Wun
Saint Paul	Corpus	Anima	Spiritus

THE THREE PRINCIPLES OF MAN
Table of correspondence of the names in various schools and traditions.

In order to facilitate the reduction to the Ternary of the Seven Terms, we are going to borrow from Barlet a key of the Classification in seven Principles which will be very useful to those who wish to return to the natural Division in synthesizing the details of analysis. (One will find the details of analysis in the *Traité élémentaire de science occulte*, 5th edition.)

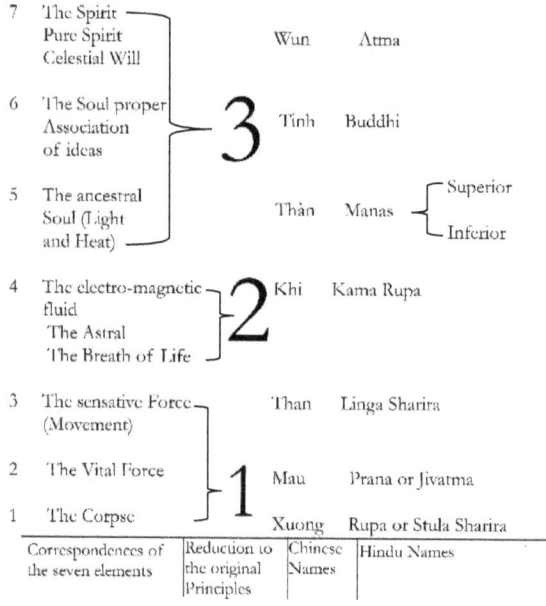

CONCLUSION

The majority of the debates which are raised between men who think on the great problems which trouble humanity arise from a confusion of terms or from a lack of observation.

In this rapid exposé of the constitution of the human being, we have avoided the extreme detail as much as dogmatic assertions.

It is to the most elementary anatomy, it is to the first rudiments of physiology, it is finally to the current observation that we have addressed ourselves to seek the solution of our problem.

And all the sciences questioned respond to us that *Man is a Trinity synthesized in an admirable Unity*.

Man, as have asserted the old sages of ancient Egypt, as have maintained especially the Kabbalists and the Hermetic philosophers, as declares Saint Paul, is therefore triple and one, made in the image of the creative word, of the divine Christ whose human form proclaims the law.

Let us leave, then, the classical philosophers and the theologians to wonder whether an intermediary term between the principle of matter which is the body and the divine principle which is the immortal spirit is necessary to beauty or equilibrium of reasoning. Nature responds brutally to this question by the fact, in establishing *special organs* for the action of this intermediary principle that we call: *the astral body*, but which has received a multitude of other names.

Physical Body, Soul, Spirit, such is the trinity of the constitution of the human being that we strove to our best to elucidate.

One will find, furthermore, great details in the special works on the question cited at the end of this account. Likewise, we are waiting to soon publish other studies on the invisible world and on the faculties only little studied here of the astral body.

While waiting, we will be happy to receive all the observations that the imperfection of our modest essay may arouse.

Papus.

WHAT BECOMES OF OUR DEAD?

by Papus
(1914)

INTRODUCTION

In the sweetness of Peace, when existence flows tranquil and without anguish, the phenomenon of death is an accident upon which one thinks as little as possible.

But when a social cataclysm like a war comes abruptly to carry off not only the flower of humanity into the armies, but also poor women and innocent children caught by the invasion or the bombardment, or abruptly devoured in an act of piracy inconceivable for a normal brain, then Death becomes a captivating problem which merits a serious and thoughtful study.

Yet, the research relative to this phenomenon, so important for humanity, has been abandoned to groups generally operating with preconceived ideas.

For the materialists, Death is a total disappearance of the individual, followed by a physical and chemical transformation of its constitutive elements.

For the religious, death is the ascension to that paradise expressed by the believers.

Between these two extreme schools is constituted, little by little and with great difficulty, an experimental school which endeavors to study the problem of the afterlife like all the current problems of biology and transcendental psychology.

The author would wish, in this small work, to make his efforts to set forth as impartially as possible the various aspects of this question according to all the Schools. But the author does not hide that, personally, he is convinced of the human being beyond death, and of the possibility, in certain cases, to establish a relation between the plane where live the "dead of the Earth" and the plane where cry and suffer the inhabitants of said Earth.

This declaration being made so as not to let this work be considered as the compilation of a skeptic, the author will make every effort not to offend any opinion, and to present as best as possible the arguments that he regards the most clear and the most scientifically established.

Papus

THE FAMILIAL FORTRESS

Poor beings, today despondent, you have constructed your social position with patience. Thanks to your privations, the son was assured of the tranquility of his material life, your daughter, raised on good principles, had a substantial dowry that she generated herself with intelligence...

Your little social and familial fortress was egotistically protected against all risks. Stock shares, multiple insurance policies, valuable real estate, all contributing to removing from you those hours of anguish in which flounder the improvident artists, the under-employed, and the needy of every kind.

But abruptly the thunder-clap is come: war! Your son, who was going to receive his architect degree, departs bravely as a non-commissioned officer. This is a Frenchman. Your son-in-law, married for barely six months, departs as a soldier of the infantry...

And the familial fortress has disappeared, and the hours of anguish have begun. It is then that the women, the Mother and daughter, have shown their hearts to be in full bloom. They have helped the other women more unfortunate than themselves materially, but not morally, for anguish grips equally all those who have one of their own... over there.

And the days had succeeded one another, intersected by the rare news of the combatants.

Then the letters from the son have abruptly stopped. Your dear mailings are returned with the notice, "This package could not join the addressee." Then an official news brief: Sergeant X... is considered "Missing" at such date, in such place...

The torment then begins: search for comrades being able to furnish any detail whatever, you know that they have seen him fall, wounded, the head of his section... The silence in response to all your measures... The rash hypotheses haunt your imagination night and day.

Finally, to put an end to it all, official news of the death of your son-in-law, the very next day after his wife announced to him an impending birth, and all three of you find yourselves face to face with two terrible powers: Destiny, implacable and unknown, *Death*...What becomes of the current life, before the dominating appearance of these forces on which one has never thought?

The individual has disappeared before the collectivity. The family has disappeared before the social, and each human atom has been taken out of orbit to become a cell of defense of the Fatherland in danger.

Why this implacable destiny?
What becomes of our dead?

This is what we are now going to ask those that were already deeply interested in the questions before the war. Each division of our study will correspond to one of the parts of the ancient sphinx: the Eagle, Man, Lion, and Bull.

Exegesis of the Soul

CHAPTER I

SECTION OF THE EAGLE

Feminine Intuition - The Ideal

The reasoning and skeptical brain of man has need of dry arguments, specified and supported upon facts.

But for you, mothers, spouses, sisters who weep for a missing loved one, this argument is useless.

Your intuition suffices.

Guardians of the most subtle forces of Nature, something resides within us, which speaks louder and more clearly than all the complicated reasoning of men.

You sense and you know that the "dear departed" are here around us. They come in a dream too often repeated to embrace the mother or the beloved spouse... the small child that the terrestrial forces have not yet entirely engrossed, also sees "upon the two planes" and he sees the state of watchfulness of "papa soldier" that the mother weeps for secretly.

Hallucinations, nervous troubles, madness, says the scholar... But the woman feels strongly that there are realities here higher than the terrestrial realities.

The sick dog let go into the country-side finds the herb necessary to its healing, and yet the poor beast has not wasted his time in any school. But a force circulates in him, more infallible than the science of many humans, and this force is the intelligence of Nature that the profane call: Instinct.

Now, you are the sacred guardians of this formative intelligence of Nature, O women, in all the social classes.

Listen, then, from the depths of your heart, to the murmur of that mysterious voice which is perceptible only to you...

Recall that the same voice long ago enchanted your heart as a young girl when your fiancée spoke to you during long and unforgettable walks.

Then, when the baby is born, even before it can speak, the sweet and mysterious voice made itself heard again often...

And now, in the greatest depths of sorrow, the voice cries again: No, mother, your son has not disappeared without recourse... The creator is the Divine Father, and a Father is never an executioner.

He is fallen for *all the others,* and by this he is become one of the lights of the invisible heavens... A curtain separates him from you, and your love will know how to make this curtain rise... Courage, woman overwhelmed by sorrow; hope, pray, and keep for yourself alone the words of the voice...

Let your heart be closed to the profane and to the profaners, send the scholars and the skeptics back to their studies... and call the missing loved one, pray those who are up there to enlighten you, and the sweet Virgin of Light will extend upon you her veil of celestial purple and astral gold... and behind this veil your dear departed will smile upon you and bless you.

Women of the Earth, glorious or crucified, be blessed, as you deserve it!

It is to you, then, that I appeal first of all, O women who have lost a dear being: son, husband, or close relative; it is to you whose intuition has not been deformed by the incomplete science of the age that I address myself. Do you not know well that the loved being has not disappeared forever? Do you not feel the truth of the assertion of all the religions of the earth, and especially of your own, when they tell you that Death is only a momentary transformation?

You have the certainty at the foundation of your being that you will see the missing again, all the more surely that he has voluntarily sacrificed himself for his country.

And this mysterious intuition is the relief of the truth itself; the disappeared has changed state, but he is still himself, even more elevated because of his sacrifice He is still bound to the beings remaining on Earth by the Love which is imperishable; a simple curtain separates him therefrom, and this curtain may sometimes be lifted.

May your heart be calmed, therefore; may the painful anguish quit your being and may you be confident and strong, woman that Nature has elected to preserve its most precious forms and its most secret germs. Dry your tears, for the one that you weep for is not far away. He is like a traveler walking in a new country and not yet being able to communicate easily with those who have remained…over there.

Seek in the calm of the Spirit to perceive the radiance of his love. Feel well as he surrounds with his presence his little children and all those whom he has left. Ask ardently of the Beings more enlightened than us to help you. Pray according to the ritual of your Religion and then it will perhaps be given to you to see the departed again from here below, for Death no longer has terror for whoever knows the Mysteries, and is then but a simple change where the Earth reclaims the body that it had lent to the Spirit for an existence, and where the Spirit, free and clothed in a new, more subtle body, evolves in a new plane.

Pray, therefore, and the veil will be lifted for you.

We are now going to endeavor to explain to you these terms: *Spirit, Subtle Body, Plane,* and later we will return to this explanation for the closed minds of the reasoning men and skeptics. Let them consider for the moment these pages as a sweet revery, they are not written for them.

CHAPTER II

SECTION OF THE MAN

Constitution of the Human Being - Death and the Evolution of the Three Principles - The Human Brain and its Evolution - The Skeptics Become Believers.

I

Constitution of the Human Being

It would be impossible to understand anything of what we say on the transformation of the human being after death, were we not to speak now on its constitution during life. Listen well, we will not enter into any detail concerning the demonstration of our statements, since large volumes are dedicated by a multitude of schools to this question.

To be clear on what is our principal aim, we will recall that the human being was considered by the ancient initiates as uniting during terrestrial life three principles or elements of constitution:
1. The Physical Body, furnished by the Earth for an existence, and attached
2. to this earth through food, by means of which it sees to the growth, then to the maintenance of this physical body.
3. Life, which is like a spark bursting between the two poles of the constitution of Man: the Body below, the Spirit above. Life is attached by the Breathing of the terrestrial atmosphere, and the terrestrial atmosphere is attached to the Light of the Sun which activates it. Breathing, therefore, attaches man to the forces emanated from the Stars, of which the Sun is the center of direction.

Also has Life received a multitude of names which rather confuses the poor beginner in these studies. Saint Paul called it the soul (*Corpus, Anima, and Spiritus*), the Spiritist Schools call it the perispirit; the Occultists, the Astral Body... and we would not be done even if we were to cite the Hebrew, Egyptian, Chinese, and Sanskrit names given to this principle of Life which has interested all seekers.

a) The immortal spirit, attached by the Intuition, the Sensibility, and the Will, to the forces of the Invisible Plane.

During the terrestrial Life, these three principles are intimately united with one another. The spirit is freed during sleep and allows Life to cleanse the body and make the organs run which depend directly on the organic Life.

Let us summarize: three principles constitute incarnate Man:
The Physical Body, Life, and Spirit.
The Physical Body attached to the Earth; Life attached to the stars, to the universal life; Spirit attached to the Superior Forces and to the Divine Plane.

Let us leave aside all the analyses of these constitutive Principles in seven, nine, or twenty one elements. This changes nothing with the question, and serve only to confuse rather clarify things.

What happens with our three principals at the moment of Death?
The vital spark is extinguished and the life, or rather the vital force, is grouped into two poles:

a) One part, more luminous, remains around the Spirit and forms the astral chariot, the chariot of the soul (Pythagoras), the subtle body which envelops the spirit in the plane of the Stars;

b) Another part, more obscure, remains in the physical body become a corpse.

The corpse returns to the earth, as a used garment returns to the second-hand dealer. The moths may destroy the clothes, as the earth may reclaim its goods at will, but this corpse is attached only by a very subtle bond to the Spirit which inhabited it.

It is not the corpse that must be venerated, it is all that the departed being has left of love and thoughts upon the Earth.

Finally, the Spirit guards its complete personality. The shock of the passage from one plane to the other rather obscures it faculties for a moment, but he is surrounded by all his own who have departed before him; if he has died for the collectivity, he is helped more by spiritual beings who deliver him from every possible suffering; and if it is necessary to weep for someone, it is certainly for the poor blind ones upon the earth and not for this spirit freed through sacrifice and illuminated by the offering of his terrestrial life in view of saving the collectivity of his country.

Such is the teaching of the Sanctuaries for more than seven thousand years. This personal existence after terrestrial life, all the initiates were sure of it, because *they have seen it*, experientially. Initiation into the mysteries of Isis had no other aim, in its elementary part, and the Initiation into all the Mysteries in all lands had the same objective.

In Sanskrit they call it "Dwidja" or "living on the two planes" the one who knows these truths practically.

It is therefore as a result of a judgment in the scientific studies or a deformation of these studies that certain minds may believe in good faith that all that becomes of man after death is cabbage, carrots, or wild flowers.

Nature is the most meticulous of the misers, and she would not have spent centuries having a human mind evolve, in order to annihilate in a minute the slow and progressive effort of so many years.

The human spirit survives physical death, and everything leads us to verify this assertion.

II

Death and the Evolution of the Three Principles

We have not all been in China, and yet we do not doubt the effective Existence of this land, because we have confidence in the travelers who return from there and who speak of it, and in a multitude of other proofs which give us the certainty that China exists.

But when it is a question of the other planes of existence, our certainty is rather diminished. The skeptics say: no one has ever returned to tell what happens over there... And the skeptics are wrong, for certain pale voyagers have returned to speak to us… And then all that touches this plane of a new existence in a body other than the physical causes fear in minds ill-prepared for the calm understanding of the realities, whatever they be, and they say to themselves: when I get there, I will see indeed.

By contrast, those who are still in the physical plane, those who remain on this side while the dear beings are departed, would wish to know… would wish to have the minutest details, and it is for them that we write these pages.

We know first that if, for a scholar initiated into the ancient mysteries of Egypt, the phases of Death were as known as those of Birth for a Physician, since initiation consisted rightly in acquiring a clear idea, practically, of these phases; for a contemporary mind, it is completely otherwise.

The psychic sciences are in phase of constitution from the point of view of the scientific bodies called "serious." Certain specialists from the Academies dedicated to this research admit that there is "something," but without going so far as the assertions of the Spiritists or Occultists.

We maintain, therefore, to henceforth state well the character of our work and to say that certain of our assertions derive from our experiences and our personal studies, although we have the certitude that all this will be "scientific" in twenty years, as it was scientific around the year 2,600 BC.

The phenomenon of death appears to us, from a purely physiological point of view, as characterized by the following facts:

1. Breaking of the equilibrium of the forces which produced the vital spark;
2. Splitting of the human being into two sections: a) the corpse; b) another body more subtle than the corpse, and which is extricated from this latter;
3. Possible manifestation and evolution of the intellectual faculties remaining in this second fluidic body, after the forced shock caused to these faculties by the phenomenon of Death…

III

The Human Mind and its Evolution

The human brain is an organ which evolved like all the other organs. It digests the ideas and personalizes thoughts, as the stomach digests food and prepares it to form the personalized human substance.

There are brains of every age among men of a different age: a man of sixty years who has never utilized his intellectual faculties may have a mind of a ten- year-old; whereas an artist of twenty-one years who has already suffered and who has created his personality through trials may have the mind of a fifty-year-old. There are minds which radiate and minds which absorb.

Finally, there are different stages in the development of the functions of the brain:

First of all, the human being is not differentiated from the mass: he believes what they tell him to believe, he does not, by a new digestion, ripen the ideas that they serve him all ready. If the teaching that he has received is religious, he believes in religious ideas; if, on the contrary, the first teaching is irreligious and takes its source in the dailies with demagogic tendencies or in the popular pamphlets, then this being does not believe anything outside of material life and his amelioration by "the struggle of the classes." We do not criticize anything, we state.

In the second stage of cerebral development begins the creation of the intellectual personality.

The individual denies first of all what he has learned in the first stage. If he has been raised in a believing environment, he suddenly becomes as unbeliever, and he is only really capable of evolving when he has become entirely materialist and atheist.

It is from the middle of this cerebral darkness, this negation of all acquired previously that will come later the red belief, reasoned and personal. But it is necessary beforehand that the brain organize itself and pass through the phases of: doubt, negation, materialism, then positivism, creation of a personal system, and finally: belief reasoned and derived from the facts and from individual thoughts.

The materialist feels that his brain is more evolved than that of the believer from the outset, but the materialist imagines that he is also more evolved than the believer by personal creation, and that is his error.

In order to have a clear idea of the effective existence of these different stages of cerebral evolution, it suffices to read with care the life of Auguste Comte, the creator of positivism, who had become a mystic at the end of his days, through normal evolution of the brain, and this to the great scandal of his disciples, remaining on the path, who believed him mad.

IV

Skeptics Become Believers.

There exists a whole library of books dedicated to the problem that we only outline here.

In an excellent booklet *L'au-delà et la survivance de l'être*, the author, Leon Denis[1], well known by all psychists, writes with respect to the skeptics become believers some lines that we are pleased to cite while referring the reader to the entire work:

"Is there not one singular thing? Never, perhaps have they seen a collection of facts, considered at first as impossible, the idea of which raised in the thoughts of the majority of men only antipathy, mistrust, disdain, which were exposed to the hostility of several secular institutions, ending up associating itself to the attention and even the conviction of educated men, of competent scholars, authorized by their functions and their character.

"These men, at first skeptics, have come from there, through their studies, their research, their experiments, to recognize and assert the reality of the majority of the spiritist phenomena.

"Sir William Crookes, the greatest physicist of modern times, after having observed for three years the materializations of the spirit of Katie King and having them photographed, has declared: 'I do not say: this is possible; I say, this is.'

"They have claimed that W. Crookes has recanted. Now, he has responded himself to this insinuation in his opening discourse to the Congress of Bristol, as president of the *British Association for the Advancement of the Sciences*. Speaking on the phenomena that he has described, he added: 'I have nothing to retract, I hold to my declarations already published. I could even add much to it.'

"Russel Wallace, of the Royal Academy of London, in his work entitled: *The Miracle and Modern Spiritualism*, has written: 'I was a materialist so perfect and so tested that I could not, at that time, find place in my thoughts for the concept of a spiritual existence. The facts, nevertheless, are stubborn things; the facts have won me over.'

"The professor Hyslop, of the University of Columbia, New York, in his report on the mediumship of Mrs. Piper entranced, said:

"'To judge it according to what I have seen myself, I do not know how I could escape the conclusion that the existence of a future life is absolutely demonstrated.'

"F. Myers, professor at Cambridge, in his beautiful work: *La Personnalité humaine*[2], arrives at this conclusion: 'That voices and messages return to us from beyond the grave.'

"Speaking on Mr. Thompson, he adds: 'I believe that the majority of these messages come from spirits, who temporarily make use of the organism of the mediums to give them to us.'

"Richard Hodgson, president of the *American Society of Psychical Research* wrote in the *Proceedings of the Society of Psychical Research*: 'I believe, without having the least doubt, that the communicating spirits are indeed the personalities whom they say to be; that they have survived the change that we call death, and that they have communicated directly with us, the so-called living, through the intermediary of the organism of Mrs. Piper sleeping.'

"The same Richard Hodgson, deceased in December, 1906, has communicated since with his friend James Hyslop, entering into minute details on the subject of the experiments and works of the Society of Psychical Research. He explains how it was necessary to lead them in a manner to prove his identity[3].

"These communications are transmitted by different mediums who did not know each other, and they corroborated one another. They recognized the words and phrases which were familiar to the communicant during his life.

"Sir Oliver Lodge, Rector of the University of Birmingham and member of the Royal Academy, writes, in *The Hilbert Journal*, what follows (reproduced by the *Light*, July 8, 1911):

"'Speaking for my account and with the sentiment of my responsibility, I have to state that as a result of my investigation into psychism, I have in the long run and quite gradually acquired the conviction, and am now convinced, after more than twenty years of studies, not only that the persistence of personal existence is a fact, but that a communication may occasionally, but with difficulty and in special conditions, reach us across space.'

"And in the conclusion of his recent book: *La Survivance humaine*[4], he adds:

"'We do not come to announce an extraordinary news; we do not bring any means of communication, but simply a collection of proofs of identity carefully established by developed methods, though ancient, more exact and closer to perfection, perhaps, than those obtained up to now. I say "proofs carefully established," for the ingenuity with which they have been prepared to meet, as much from the other side of the barrier as from ours. There has distinctly been cooperation between those who are in the material and those who are not.'

"The Professor W. Barrett, of the University of Dublin, declares (*Annals of the Psychical Sciences*, November and December, 1911):

"'Without doubt, for our part, we believe that there is some active intelligence at work behind automatism (mechanical writing, trance, and incorporations) and outside of this an intelligence, which is more probably the deceased person that it asserts to be, than any other thing that we may imagine... It is difficult to find another solution to the problem of these messages and these *increased correspondences*, without imagining an attempt of intelligent cooperation between certain disincarnate spirits and our own.'

"The celebrated Lombroso, professor at the University of Turin, wrote in his *Lettura*:

"'I am forced to formulate my conviction that the spiritist phenomena are of an enormous importance, and that it is the duty of science to direct its attention without delay to these manifestations.'

"Mr. Boutroux, member of the Institute and professor at the Faculty of Arts of Paris, expresses himself in this way in the *Matin* on March 14, 1908:

"'A large study, complete, on *psychism* offers not only an interest of curiosity, even scientific, but also concerns very directly the life and destiny of individuals and humanity.'

"The scholar Mr. Duclaux, director of the Pasteur Institute, in a conference made to the General Psychological Institute some years ago, said: 'I do not know if you are like me, but this world populated by influences that we go through without knowing, permeated by this *quid divinum* that we perceive without having detail of, well! This world of psychism is a world more interesting than the one which has until now confined our thought. Let us try to open it to our research. There are immense discoveries to make there which will benefit humanity.'"

All these citations are applied by the positivists ready to pass from the personal system, which they have made, to a whole series of reasoned beliefs which will lead them little by little to that state of mind that the oriental schools compare to a tranquil water, in which may be reflected and attained by the consciousness of the waking state, all the teachings received by the human Spirit in the *Invisible Planes of Nature*.

This evolution of beliefs may, which is rare, be realized in a single human life, as in the case of August Comte; or, more frequently, requiring several existences.

In the first stage, while man is content to admit, without debating them, the ideas that are presented to him, one may place all the beings capable of blind belief, and the slightly superstitious, such as, for example, the belief in Saint Anthony of Padua to find a lost object, may find a place, and all those, finally, who follow mechanically according to a primitive impulse the precepts of any religion.

In the second, the mind begins to want to know the limits of its domain, it penetrates into the land of doubt and negation. One may place there all those great intelligences who have not yet encountered their path, and who, from Galileo to Tolstoy, have astonished the world by the constant struggle of their genius with the terrible, immutable, and unique truth.

As prototype of the mind which has penetrated into the cold equilibrium of the third stage, that of pure Materialism, which is often fatalistic, we will indicate the positivistic and atheistic physician, having never found the soul under his scalpel, no more, besides, than the mechanic finds the telegraphist by dismantling an apparatus, or the violinist by breaking the violin. The materialist physician coldly denies all that does not fall into his mental logic. Even if his heart came to suddenly register a living and marvelous truth, his brain would be closed and not let pass into his consciousness this strange truth. The facts which do not enter into his way of thinking are purely and simply rejected without examination.

Then, under the influence of a suffering, perhaps, come the "new glimmers"; the Positivist no longer recoils before the facts most contrary to his way of thinking, but he studies them in an impartial manner: let us cite here the names of Lodge, Myers, Russell Wallace, Lambroso, Charles Richet, etc.

Here, now, is the fifth stage, in which we will classify all the minds who have succeeded by the study of the facts in creating for themselves a personal system more or less bringing together the teachings of the tradition. Little by little they are led, no longer by blind belief, but by experiential reasoned belief.

It is then, in all its degrees, the direct knowledge by the heart of the great spiritual truths; but it is at the same time the reception into the brain of these grandiose truths. It is the perfect equilibrium between the feminine and masculine faculties of the human being. The marvelous light of Faith illuminates then the cerebral cells, which, in their turn, adapt to the physical life, sometimes by concealing with a necessary veil, the spiritual knowledge reaching it.

Then, finally, the physical organism of man constitutes for its directing principle: the soul, a perfect instrument. The cerebral Evolution has ended for the earth.

Papus

CHAPTER III

SECTION OF THE LION

The three planes - The forces in the three planes - Communication between the planes - Experimentation - Union of the Visible and the Invisible - The errors and traps - Active Faith and Prayer

I

The Notion of the Planes

When one reads for the first time the works of the writers who have dedicated themselves to the study of the invisible forces, one is hindered by a multitude of technical terms. By pursuing one's readings and verifying one author by another, one quickly comes to understand this special jargon and one sees oneself very well in the terms: perispirit, metapsychical forces, astral body, astral plane, mental plane, manasic Kama forces, superior spirits, etc., etc...

There are, however, upon which we believe we must henceforth insist, among others that of *planes*.

Let us put into a test-tube:
1. Some Mercury;
2. Some Water;
3. Some Oil.

These three substances do not mix. They form in the glass three layers or planes.

If we suppose these substances inhabited by living beings: lower plants, bacteria, or others, we will have:

The inhabitants of the plane of Mercury below;

The inhabitants of the plane of Water in the middle;

Finally, the inhabitants of the plane of Oil above.

All these beings and all these substances are in the same glass and yet they do not communicate with one another: they are separated by the Density of each of the environments where they evolve.

Now, the occultists have divided Nature into three slices or planes corresponding to the image that we have just analyzed.

Below, there is the *material plane* formed of all that is visible and materialized as much upon the Earth as in all the planets; this is the plane of the physical bodies and physical forces.

Above or within this plane, exists the plane of the vital forces, the animating forces. The life which circulates in our body is an example of this force. Now, this life, according to the teachings of the ancient Egyptian science, this vital force which circulates within us, is the same force which circulates in the stars. Thus have they given the name of *astral forces* to the forces of this plane, itself named: *astral plane*.

Above still, we find the plane of the spiritual forces, of the Personality, of the

Will which repels or accepts the proofs, and finally of all the manifestations of the immortal *spirit* tied directly to the divine plane.

We have explored here the expressions: below, in the middle, above, only to satisfy the customs of our mind.

In reality, the various planes are *within* one another, they permeate one another without being mingled, like a ray of Sun passing through a window without being intimately connected with it, like the blood circulating in the body while still being enclosed within its vessels.

There is not, therefore, any special place to seek, any physical place where are cantoned the Dead of the Earth. The tradition teaches indeed that certain beings charged with matter, after their death, are cantoned in the cones of shadow that each planet trails after it in the heavens, but his is an exception. In general, our dead are in the same place as us, but in *another plane* of this place, as the oil, water, and mercury are *in the same glass*, and yet they mingle even less than the planes of the visible and invisible which, themselves, permeate one another completely.

It is therefore through a regrettable confusion that certain authors have wished to "lodge" the dead in some place of the *physical plane*. They have placed them at the center of the Earth, then in the other planets, then in the various suns. It is clear that all this is possible, but in the astral plane of these different places and not in the physical plane which is reserved to the physical bodies, materialized and incarnated.

But can one make a being to pass momentarily from the invisible or astral plane into the visible or physical plane? This is the great question of the evocations on which we will presently say some words, but we must still insist a little on this notion of the planes, for it is important to give as clear an idea as possible.

The notion of the planes plays, indeed, a considerable role in the study of the psychical problems, and much confusion or inventions without significance arise precisely from the obscurity on this notion of the planes.

Thus, every being of the physical plane, every incarnated and materialized being can only be contained in a cube, or rather in three dimensions; which means in clear language that when one wishes to "put in irons" a street ruffian, he must be put between four walls with a solid door, a ceiling to prevent escape and likewise a floor. Cage for flies or prison cell, it is a cube or a form with three dimensions, which is necessary to contain a being of the physical plane: fly or ruffian.

May our readers yet little accustomed to our jargon excuse us now if we are not very clear; we will seek as best we can to explain presently.

If I want to enclose a ray of sun, a ray of star, my cube will serve for nothing; if it is constituted as a fly-cage, the sun will pass through; if it is a quesiton of a prison cell, it will pass through the windows, even thick ones, without letting itself be seized.

But if I use a photographic plate, a ray of sun is going to decompose the silver salts and fixes the plate with the images that color it.

A surface plane, a mathematician's plane, suffices here to retain an astral ray.

Now, Occultism teaches that special beings circulate in all the rays of the stars; these beings have no physical bodies, but a body of luminous rays called an *astral body*... The plane upon which these beings live is called the *astral plane*.

In order to contain these beings, a surface plane suffices, formed by the meeting of two or three lines.

Finally, if I have an idea that I do not want to communicate with anyone, I keep it to myself, lurking in *a point* of my brain and this is a little spiritual being which will serve me later to my liking.

This spiritual being can, by the use of the Word, go move a hundred cerebral points similar to mine. Carried upon the verbal chariot, the idea has multiplied and revivified itself. Then, neither prison, nor cube, nor plane may contain it. Its essence is liberty.

That is the character of the *spiritual plane* or plane of the divine beings, of which our spirit is a spark.

To conclude: there is *a physical plane* with physical beings, furnished with a physical body and which the cube or three-dimensional construction is the necessary lodging: room, palace, or prison (space with three dimensions).

There is an *astral plane* with astral beings, furnished with an astral body and of which the surface plane is the necessary lodging (space with two dimensions).

There is a *spiritual plane* with spirits furnished with a spiritual body and of which the mathematical point is the necessary lodging (here, time and space no longer act).

Let us look, now, at how one may study, in their respective plane, the physical, astral, and spiritual forces, We will limit ourselves to some general ideas quite sufficient for the aim that we pursue.

II

The Forces in the Three Planes

The physical forces are easy to study, since they function on our plane.

One may occupy oneself, say, with the hydrolic forces with their large instruments, from the wheel of the mill to the conduit of the modern works of "water-power."

One may study as well the water vapor circulating in its slender pipes.

One may even describe the electricity in circulation within the metallic wires.

These are all modalities of the physical force.

In general, this force presents the following characteristics:
1. Necessity of a conductive material;
2. Dynamism in relation with the condensation or materialization of the force;
3. Modifications produced upon the inert matter by the action of the material forces.

The study of an astral force may be pursued by following the modalities of the Light of the Sun acting upon the Earth.

This force is first animated with a considerable quickness of displacement (more than 200,000 kilometers per second). It thus traverses immense spaces with the greatest rapidity.

This force becomes dynamic only if it is condensed by means of resistance. Mirrors will allow the effective heat to be drawn from it; one may also, by means of special condensers, draw electricity therefrom. But normally, the light of the Sun passes through glass without shattering it, and thus indicates the character of an astral force which is to pass through the material forces without disturbing the latter.

Finally, as the solar force is the same as the vital force which circulates in all the living beings, this solar force is a physiologically restorative power.

Such are the general characteristics of an astral force.

We do not have to discuss here the real origin of the solar light. Whether this light actually comes from the Sun, as teaches current Astronomy, or whether it be, on the contrary, produced in the atmosphere of our planet by an emanation of neutral solar force which is transformed into light, heat, and electricity at the contact of each planet matters little. What interests us presently is following an astral force in action upon the Earth. For the rest, the scientists are there to resolve these questions of origin, ever obscure, and always too technical to be approached in a wholly elementary study.

The forces of the *intellectual* and *spiritual plane* are still little known by the contemporaries. The initiatic colleges of Antiquity and certain mysterious societies of India, of Islam, and also of the Occident have had some precise notions thereof.

The forces of this plane act outside of Time and Space. They are transmitted instantaneously from one planet to another as well as between two points very far removed from the Earth.

In order to manifest themselves, these forces have need of a point of material support. They utilize in general the nervous organs and the brain of living beings.

It is therefore an error to believe that "chains of will" may act directly upon social events.

Chains of physical light could endeavor as well to break material windows. The light passes through the window without destroying anything; the Thought passes through the astral stereotypes without direct influence.

It is therefore very important to avoid this error of the action of spiritual forces without material tool.

Joan of Arc would not have been able to do anything without an army. This army had accomplished miracles since its constitution, but it was necessary because upon the material plane, one can act dynamically only by means of material forces.

A human being who has passed into the spiritual plane no longer has any direct action over matter. he passes through objects like the light passes through the window, and he must utilize special tools like the vital force of a human medium, or some particular resistance like glass and wood, in order to put himself in contact with this material plane from which he is so removed.

III

Communications Between the Various Planes

To cause a being to pass from one plane to another is an act in which it is necessary to momentarily counteract the laws of Nature. That is why this kind of experiment is delicate, dangerous, and full of traps and fraud.

In order to give a clear idea of the problem to be resolved, we will relate in what conditions physical beings may be found in the sections of the physical plane, different for each of them by their condition of normal existence.

Thus, there is a fish who can only live in water. If we want to place it in the air, which is the element where we men live, we are going to be obliged to find an intermediary between the air and water, which, in the case of our fish, will be a glass receptacle containing water.

But if we want in our turn to go visit the land of the fish, an intermediary will be necessary for us, containing the air that is our land, our plane, and this intermediary will be a diver's outfit, which will be for us as the fishbowl for the fish.

These images are intended to make it understood that in order to cause a being of the astral plane, like a dead person, or rather like the Spirit of a being dead to the Earth, to pass into the physical plane, it is necessary to find the necessary intermediaries.

These intermediaries are constituted by vital forces placed at the disposal of the Spirit evoked, and by material objects on which the Spirit may condense the forces put at its disposal.

A little history seems to us indispensible here.

Recall the History of Ulysses related by Homer. Wanting to seek the counsel of his old friend Tiresias, prophet of his trade, Ulysses is informed that Tiresias is dead.

Anyone else would have left here any plan of conversation, but the hero of Homer is not stopped by so little.

He is dead, indeed, *we are going to make him return.*

Ulysses then descends into the astral planes that the ancients called the inferior planes, *Infera*, the Underworld.

There he prepares his experiment. (Re-read it in the text.) He traces a circle with his sword, astral figure which will surround him and prevent the beings of the astral plane from approaching to close to him.

Then Ulysses puts into play the force charged with being the intermediary between the two planes. This force is the blood of a young goat slaughtered in the circle.

This is the medium or mediumistic force of all the initiates of Antiquity, the blood or visible force of the Animals.

The fluids which escape from the blood attract the spirits in droves. Ulysses dispersed them from the circle with his sword. He allowed Tiresias alone to inhale the vital fluids of the blood. Tiresias then materialized, he spoke and, passing for a moment from the astral or invisible plane into the physical or visible plane, he gave to Ulysses the necessary counsels.

IV

Experimentation - Union of the Visible and the Invisible – The Errors and Traps

When one perceives the notion that it is possible to communicate from one plane to the other, the craziest hopes arise. They imagine that with any human intermediary or medium, the veil is then going to be raised and that they will have some words or news from their dear departed.

Certainly not. It is not as easy as may be imagined by the enthusiasts of the first hour who are going towards certain delusions and most cruel despair.

As it is a question here of an experiment of true science, it is necessary to proceed very methodically. One may indeed communicate with difficulty:

1. With the mind of the medium, whether this medium be sleeping or not.

By means of an object that is a bad conductor of electricity or vital fluid which follows nearly the same laws, for example by means of a wooden table, which has replaced the wand of the ancients, the medium unites and condenses the life of the person consulted with her own. Then the thoughts of the consulted are *reflected* by the intermediary or medium and the table tells the name and age of the deceased… and yet the deceased has nothing to do with this affair.

2. May they forgive us for speaking on things which are going to seem bizarre, but the necessity to avoid disillusions pushes us there. It is a question here of "astral stereotypes."

All our actions, good or evil, float around us and around the objects which surround us when we accomplished these acts. We appear then to the eyes of the seers, like the actor of a cinematograph producing scenes in color. This is what we call "astral stereotypes."

The medium may evoke one of these scenes and the consulted imagines that it is in relation to the deceased, which is not exact.

3. It is therefore in proceeding by elimination, as have done the scholars who have dedicated themselves to these studies, that one may succeed in stablishing a certain bond between the beings of the Earth and the Spirits of those who have formerly lived here below.

The communication by medium is therefore less sure than the manifestation by Dreams, and it is always to this latter that we give preference.

We encourage the serious seekers to read the collection of the *Annales des Science Psychiques*, of which Mr. de Vesme is director, and the works on *Spiritisme Scientifique* and the *Apparitions Matérialisées*, by Gabriel Delanne. After these readings, one will be well in possession of all the difficulties of the problem, and will better understand our warnings.

V

Active Faith and Prayer

Communication between the living and the dead is indeed a thing so sacred, that it is necessary to guard oneself well against attempting it lightly. Certainly, it exists, it is evident, but it ought only ever be the reward granted to goodness, to the good will. Any human being who has understood some part of the spiritual laws will not attempt voluntarily to call a deceased for fear of bringing real damage to himself; for fear also of going blindly to the encounter of cruel disillusionment.

What, then, must be done? Or rather, what may we do to elucidate this problem, unsolvable in appearance?

There are two paths: the one indirect, the other direct. In the first, we can, through the reading and study of the special works, reach a sort of intellectual belief, a sort of reasoned faith. The truly enormous number of facts well stated, the authority which is attached to the name of certain seekers, may determine in our cerebral cells a sort of favorable receptivity of the facts that we would have to state by ourselves.

But the second path, the direct and personal path, is much preferable. Two great words, two great lights illuminate this path: Active Faith, Prayer.

Faith is the intelligence of the heart. It is the perception, by an organ other than the brain, of some truth that this latter cannot arrive at by itself, but that it may reflect upon when it is illumined by the light of the heart. One characteristic of knowledge through Faith is the absolute absence of doubt, certitude in shadows. Whereas any purely mental knowledge may only rarely attain to this entire certitude.

One could compare the brain to a phonograph roll upon which would be inscribed innumerably diverse notions; at the least excitation, this roll sets itself into motion and presents any one of these notions, and this, endlessly, for as long as it lasts. If, then, we wish to reach a certainty concerning the *survival* and the communication between the living and the dead, by a strictly mental path, we have to vanquish the objections, ever new, presented to our consciousness by our brain.

On the contrary, let us calm our mental state by illuminating it through active faith; a whole series of organs will be developed within us, capable of knowing the truth of the *survival* as clearly as our eyes have consciousness of the Sun by a beautiful summer day. We know then, without possible debate, that our *me* makes at the death of the body only a change of vehicle, of instrument, and that it is eternal. At this moment, the facts observed will be truly useful and fruitful.

Practically, then, let us avoid, or at the very least make only with the greatest prudence, an evocation of the departed. Let us research the path of Goodness, of Charity. It will lead us surely to conscious communication without danger, first in dream, then in other states, with those that we have truly loved in God.

And I have also pronounced the word of Prayer, a word so poorly understood, a thing so little known.

I would come out of the limits I have traced for myself by expatiating upon this chapter; may it be permitted to me, however, to say that prayer is the living universal key. By it, man, plunged into the most complete darkness, may hope to finally see again the light which shines eternally at the summit of the Holy Hill.

By it will be opened for him the closed books of life, of death, and of rebirth.

By it the ordeal will become bearable, and the roses will appear under the thorns of the path.

By it, finally, man will one day be able to raise the veil which separates life from death, and when he will have the strength, the beloved whom he believed lost forever will appear. Let us learn, then, to let escape from our heart that living force, and let us ask for the active faith, before which all obscurity will disappear.

Exegesis of the Soul

CHAPTER IV

SECTION OF THE BULL

*What is death for the Philosopher? - The dead are voyagers -
Death for the Homeland*

I

What is Death for the Philosopher?

    The change that one believes to be brought about in the conditions of existence of the being who dies depends above all on the ideas which circulate in the brain of those who continue to live on Earth. The being who has just died follows the immutable laws fixed by Nature and he pursues his evolution without his personal beliefs having to intervene. If, as we firmly believe for our account, something of us exists in another plane, this is a fact that we will all be called, sooner or later, to verify. Why, then, quarrel with us in advance?
    The physical relations being found cut between the dead and the living, it is the latter who claim to settle the question, and it is here that the cerebral maturity of each intervenes.
    For the ones, Death is the end of all that Nature has done up until here. Intelligence, sentiment, affections, all abruptly disappear and the body becomes herb, mineral, or smoke according to the case.
    For the others, Death is a liberation. The Soul, all light, disengages itself from the corpse and flies away towards the heavens, surrounded by angels and glorious spirits.
    Between these two extreme opinions exist all the intermediary beliefs.
    The Pantheists base the Personality of the Dead in the great currents of Universal Life.
    The Mystics teach that the Spirit freed from the shackles of matter continues to live in order to endeavor to save, through its sacrifice, those who still suffer upon the earth.
    The Initiates of the various schools follow the evolution of the being in the various planes of Nature until the moment when this being returns, and according to its desire, takes a new physical body upon the Planet where he has not finished "paying" his due.
    Death for one's country frees the Spirit nearly always, from a return or from a reincarnation…
    So many opinions, so many disputes, so many polemics for a natural event of which we are assured to see the solution!
    But they will not ask us our opinion, and if it may interest the reader, we say in all loyalty: the Dead of the Earth are the Living of another plane of evolution. In our opinion, Nature is miserly and lets none of its efforts go to waste in the nothingness. The brain of an artist or a scholar represents years and years of slow evolution. Why

would this be abruptly lost? Let us leave each to digest in silence their personal ideas. *Astra inclinant non necessitant*. Let us show what we believe to be the route, not to force anyone to take it up themselves.

II

The Dead are voyagers, momentarily absent

When one of your close relatives is traveling in a distant country, you follow him by thought and your heart is calm. We would wish to give the reader this sensation that our dead have not disappeared forever, they are travelers on another plane, but they are traversing a land where we are all going normally, if we avoid despair and suicide.

"Heaven is where one puts his heart," said Swedenborg. Now, Our Lord Jesus Christ, whose name is written in the heavens since the creation of the Earth, is a Savior on all the Planes and not an executioner. He who knows the anguishes and all the sorrows, he strives to reunite into his love, and those who weep here, and those who would wish to cry out "over there": But you do not despair, we are here and our love lives in you and through you...

It is clear that, just as there is, upon the Earth, no uniformity of occupations and social rank, there are no fixed rules for evolution in what we call the Invisible Plane.

After a more or less long period of sleep, without suffering, since there is no terrestrial matter, the Spirit awakens and begins its new existence.

It attaches itself first of all to those that it has left on earth and seeks to communicate with them through dream or through some intermediary, if it finds one.

It is not necessary to force the communications between the various planes, which are always delicate and present certain dangers. When, after a sincere desire or an ardent prayer, accompanied by an act of physical, moral, or intellectual charity, it is permitted to the Spirit to manifest itself, this always takes place in a manner not to frighten the terrestrial being.

On the contrary, if one wants to force the communications, one risks being deceived by the brain of the medium who, unconsciously, repeats cherished ideas to the consulted, or by images of the departed, animated photographs floating in the astral, or by beings who use the medium to monopolize a little material existence.

It is necessary, therefore, to be able to wait for news from the traveler. It is necessary to ask with calm to obtain the certitude of their effective existence... over there, and then to think much of the traveler, to magnetize them with love
and not with despair and tears, and then, most gently, the veil will be raised, a sweet murmur will fill the heart, the shudder of the presence of the beyond will appear, and little by little a great mystery will be revealed. At this moment, it is necessary to know how to remain silent, to not deliver their secret to the profane or to the profaners.

To hope, to pray, to have confidence in the Savior and in the Virgin of Light, such is the path which leads to the *peace of the heart*.

III

Death for one's country frees the spirit at once from all suffering.

The majority of human beings have an existence divided into two sections. On the one hand, each man occupies himself with his personal life and with that of his family, when he has one; on the other hand, this same man exercises a profession or a function useful to the collectivity.

In general, it is the exterior function utilized by the collectivity which procures the material means necessary to personal life and to that of the family. This law of two planes of existence: personal and collective, is common to all Nature.

Thus, a star like our Earth has a personal life (if one considers the life of a star its movements) characterized by its rotation upon itself, and a collective life where the star is no more than a cog-wheel of the Universe when it circulates around a Sun.

To return to the human being, he can change plane, that is to say, in common language, die, for three principal reasons:

1. For himself, when he dies single, without kin, and from an accident or a banal illness;
2. For his people, when he is led to sacrifice himself to save his family;
3. For the collectivity, when he sacrifices himself voluntarily for the salvation of defense of his country.

In each of these cases, the change of plane is caused by different modalities.

The departure which ends an existence of pure egotism is slow, and the disengagement left to the personal forces is most painful.

By contrast, every sacrifice is equilibrated by an immediate assistance of intelligent forces with the planes of disengagement. Let us call these forces: Spirits, Angels, Souls of the Homeland, Idea-forces, it matters not, since the names do not affect the matter. What is important to know, is that the one who dies for others is freed of all physical suffering and released from every mental anguish when he has changed plane.

This is an application of the universal laws that the human being goes through like all living beings; for Nature, in its impassibility, a man often has no more value than a stalk of wheat, although the pride of man is often incommensurable.

Papus
EPILOGUE

Vision of Light: The Death of the Hero

An abrupt shock... an afflux of blood to the heart... the unexpected difficulties of great events of terrestrial life... a slow disappearance, or rather a sweet sleep... the calm and the shade... The brave young man comes to be killed by a bullet, just as he was coming out for the assault...

Voices around him, a landscape of light, beings of light by which the bodies travel as if they had wings... his grandmother who raised him and whose countenance has become so young... then consoling voices and beautiful figures as in the images: Angels or Saints perhaps?

In what state, then, is found the combatant just now? Where is he? What are these strange landscapes where all is light? His body itself is luminous, tapering and traveling without touching any ground on the desire of his will... He is guided, moreover, by all the beings who surround him and who sing his coming...

My mother, I want to see you again my mother!!

At once, guided by a luminous spirit, the combatant plunges into darkness. He finds himself abruptly in the cherished lodging of long ago, but he can never hold on... he passes through the walls, as through all the objects... and no one perceives his presence.

He sees his dear mother anguished... he throws himself towards her and this impetus of love makes a miracle... His mother sees him, but she faints while crying: "My son, my son is dead... he just appeared to me..."

Then the Spirit of the child remains around the beloved being left upon the Earth; he wants to tell her that Death is not a suffering for him, that the despair of those who weep for his departure is the only trouble that he has known... but the words are not heard.

Only the radiance of his love surrounds with light the beautiful invisible being of this woman who has given her son to the country, and who, remembering the martyr of Mary, the mother of O.L. Jesus, asks heaven the strength to endure this atrocious sorrow.

The following night, the child communicates in a dream with his beloved mother and tells her: Do not cry, for I am always near you: those that they believe dead, are the guides over there... courage and hope, when your task will be finished on Earth, I will come to seek you, as grandmother has come for me.

Dry your tears and be strong: you have merited well from your Father, be blessed.

Exegesis of the Soul

THE YOUNG SOLDIER

At Chaumon-sur-Argonne, near Pierrefille, in a trench, a young German was dead, holding near his head and at the height of his eyes his book of prayers…

Poor victim of the madness of the great, I salute you and I join my prayers to those which have illumined your Spirit at the moment of your departure. Sensing the death to come, you have bravely prepared your soul for the physical separation, and obscure hero, you have called out to the One who hears us all… May your gesture be blessed. What does it matter that you are the enemy of my country and an envoy of the prideful who have sacrificed the flower of their men to the base satisfaction of their ambition.

Little grain of sand in this immense conflict, you have gone, you have obeyed, and you have just been physically crushed in some trench in the middle of the fields of France and near some woods… But if your body is returned to that Earth which has nourished it and made it grow, your Spirit, over which no material force has hold, has been freed and raised, glorious, into the Empyrean plane.

In the heart of Our Lord, there are no longer either friends or enemies when the terrible Death has passed, there are no longer but Spirits who have been sacrificed for the Ideal, and who have come to their end abruptly on their terrestrial route…

And the perfume of prayer has sanctified your final moments… and I have passed and I have felt your Spirit calm in its well-earned evolution, and I too have wished to join my prayers with yours… Enemies of yesterday, let us be able to communicate today in the Ideal superior to human quarrels.

You have a family, poor little guy, a mother who is going to weep, sisters who will remember, and brothers who will perhaps imitate you.

And all, in their sorrow, are going to prostrate themselves and pray… Innocent victim of blind ambitions and profound egotism, envoy of blind barbary against the conscious and luminous evolution of the free Peoples, you have done your duty, but the unmerciful hand of Destiny has marked you with its finger and your evolution is accomplished.

Tomorrow you will return upon the earth, but you will have drunk from the Lethe… innocent victim… I salute you and I pray with you…

Nicey, September 19, 1914

NOTES

1. Léon Denis. *L'Au-delà et la survivance de l'Etre*. Paris, Durville, 1912.
2. Paris, Alcan. I, 05. In-8vo.
3. See the Proceedings S.P.R.
4. La Survivance humaine, by Sir Oliver Lodge, translated from the English by Doctor Bourbon. Paris, 1912. Félix Alcan, publisher.

www.ingramcontent.com/pod-product-compliance
Lightning Source LLC
Chambersburg PA
CBHW020921090426
42736CB00008B/736